how to become
A SUCCESSFUL MODEL

how to become

A SUCCESSFUL MODEL

by Viju Krem

A Stuart L. Daniels Book

ARCO PUBLISHING COMPANY, Inc.

New York

Second Edition, First Printing, 1978

Published by Arco Publishing Company, Inc.
219 Park Avenue South, New York, New York 10003

Copyright © 1975, 1978 by Arco Publishing Company, Inc.

Library of Congress Cataloging in Publication Data

Krem, Viju.
  How to become a successful model.

  "A Stuart L. Daniels book."
  1. Models, Fashion—Vocational guidance.   I. Title.
HD6073.M7K73   659.1'52   77-13370
ISBN 0-668-04517-5 (Library Edition)
ISBN 0-668-04508-6 (Paper Edition)

Printed in the United States of America

ACKNOWLEDGMENTS

My deep appreciation to Elizabeth Cossa for her editorial assistance.

PHOTOGRAPHY

Cover Photo: Tom Andron
Tom Andron: pages 31, 32, 36 (top)
Taylor Cushmore: pages 2, 6, 51, 68, 89 (bottom), 110 through 121, 132, 133 (bottom)
Leslie Stuart Communications: pages 8, 20, 24, 108, 122, 133 (top), 138
Wide World: 42, 67, 140
Charles Revson, Inc.: page 23
Gary Bernstein: 53, 140.

A NOTE TO THE READER

I hope this book gives you all the information you'd like to have about becoming a professional model. But I know there are many questions of a more individual nature that can't be answered in a book. If you would like to have more information concerning the field of modeling, write to me:

Viju Krem
% Arco Publishing Co., Inc.
219 Park Avenue South
New York, N.Y. 10003

contents

becoming
a model

Hello! I'm Viju Krem and I'm a professional model. In case you're wondering how to pronounce my name, (and almost everybody does,) its Vee-You, and my last name, Krem, rhymes with hem. Now that we've got that out of the way I'd like to tell you something about myself. After all, if you're going to take my advice on something as important as your career in professional modeling, you should get to know me.

You should also know why I've written this book. Hardly a week goes by that one of my friends doesn't ask me to speak to a sister or a niece or a neighbor's daughter about becoming a model. When I talk to these girls I am amazed at the misinformation they have.

There are tens of thousands of girls who would like to become models. Most of them seem to be doing the wrong things to achieve that goal. I found that some girls spend money on useless photographs because they think a modeling agency must see professional photographs. Other girls have developed some strange ideas about what a model should wear or the kinds of makeup she should use.

9

ADVICE FROM THE EXPERTS

When I decided to write a book on the subject and realized that I would need more information than my own experience provided, I talked to people in the modeling profession who really *know* what it takes to become a successful model. I talked to agency owners, casting directors, advertising executives, photographers and almost every professional model I know. While opinions vary on some points, everyone agrees about two. First, becoming a model depends on a combination of good looks, hard work and common sense. And becoming a successful model depends on drive, determination and the ability to learn from other people's mistakes and from your own.

Another reason for writing this book is that I love my profession and I'm proud of being a model. It makes me furious when I hear or read something so distorted that it insults all of us who make modeling our career. Believe me, I've heard it all. "Models are beautiful, but boy, are they dumb."

"Models are so hung up on their looks they don't think about anything else." Or the one I really despise, "Any pretty girl can be a model if she's *nice* to the right people." I wanted a chance to tell would-be models what this business is really all about.

Today, as never before, modeling itself is serious business. Models are an integral part of the commercial world. They contribute to the sale of countless billions of dollars worth of merchandise every year.

Models work in fashion, cosmetics and nearly every phase of advertising and public relations. We are as much a part of these ventures as the photographers, designers, fashion coordinators, manufacturers and distributors. In doing our job in the best way we know, each of us make a valuable contribution to these industries. With all the millions of dollars involved it seems ridiculous for people not to understand that modeling is a respectable and creative career.

Some of the advice I am going to give may surprise you. It may go against everything you've always believed to be true. A lot of it stems from plain common sense and seems so obvious that you will hear yourself saying, "Now why didn't I think of that."

If I shatter some of your fondest illusions about modeling, forgive

10

me. But I believe in the old saying, "forewarned is forearmed." So, if you're really serious about becoming a successful model—read on.

MODELS ARE MADE, NOT BORN

Would it surprise you to learn that becoming a model was *not* my childhood dream? Well, it wasn't. I don't know why most people seem to think that models are born with a set of false eyelashes in one hand and a mirror in the other.

I certainly was far removed from that. I was the biggest tomboy in my hometown, Toronto, Canada. If I ever looked in a mirror it was only during ballet class. I started dancing when I was five years old and while I now know that the training I got in those classes is invaluable to my work, modeling was not a consideration at the time. I think my mother encouraged me to dance in the hope that it would use up some of my excess energy. Today we laugh about the fact that I make a living posing for hours on end while she couldn't get me to sit still long enough to snap a picture for our family album.

When I wasn't busy dancing (and getting into anything my mother told me to stay out of), I spent much of my time with a group of girls called The Kalev-Estienne Estonian Gymnasts. Both my parents are from Estonia. I was born in Germany. Then we moved to Canada. There is a large Estonian colony in Toronto and my gymnastics group performed at Estonian rallies and picnics. We got lots of publicity and my picture was in the local papers nearly every other week (at least during the summer). A small taste of fame. I bet you think I rushed to New York to begin my career. Hardly. Especially not with a picture of me in my gym suit. What I really wanted to be was a gym teacher.

I think I was "typical" in that respect. I changed my mind every other day. If my ballet teacher said something encouraging I had visions of myself as a prima ballerina floating across a stage. I wonder if Rudolf Nureyev knows what he's missing? And after a big rally I was absolutely sure that being a gym teacher would be the greatest. Of course I had read about famous models. But they were as distant as movie stars and just as glamorous. They were the ones who had been "discovered." I had a lot to learn.

11

MODEL TRUTHS

Another popular myth about models is that they were beautiful children with aggressive parents who had pushed them right out of childhood and into their profession. While that may be true in some isolated cases, I can assure you it wasn't so with my parents. Having been brought up in Europe they had some pretty "Old World" ideas about children in general and women in particular. They were very strict. They also put great value on education. The fact that I might earn a few dollars modeling would not have influenced them to permit me to miss school.

Before you get the idea that my parents were dead set against a modeling career, let me say that today they are very proud of me. They helped and encouraged me, but only after I proved that I was serious about modeling.

Beauty, or good looks, is most often an essential ingredient in becoming a model. Not all models, however, are beautiful in the conventional sense. Some are striking or have a different or unusual appearance. Some don't look very special but exude such an appealing personality that they are just right for a certain type of product or market.

The majority of models can be considered beautiful and are often hired by a client because that beauty will attract readers or viewers to his product.

It takes a lot of courage to think that way because it goes against what most of us were taught about good manners. Being beautiful, or special, takes more, however, than just physical good looks. You have to believe that you are special inside, as well. You have to have confidence in yourself and in the thought that you make a better appearance than girls who are not models.

Some people think models are egomaniacs who believe that the sun rises and sets on them. There may be some who do, but most are modest about their physical appearance.

Whenever I make a call (we call it a go-see), and I am in the waiting room with a half a dozen other models, I can't help but notice that usually they are all beautiful. I know they want that job as much as I do. Only one will get it and the rest will be rejected.

12

Being turned down, not once, but sometimes, a dozen times in a single week doesn't do much for one's ego. But a real pro learns to accept it gracefully and faces the next job with confidence. That means that when she goes home at the end of the day she gets ready to start all over again the next morning. No self pity. No midnight orgy with a quart of chocolate ice cream because she is feeling blue and deserves a treat.

If I had to pick the toughest part of being a model, that's it. Learning to accept defeat and keep on going. We get used to getting up at the crack of dawn, standing on our feet all day, changing our clothes and fixing our makeup in all kinds of places from an unheated dressing room to a telephone booth. We learn that it is easier to watch our diet and take care of our hair, clothes and makeup before we do all the other things we'd like to do in our free time. All of this is part of the job. Still, it is not a magic success formula.

IT'S SERIOUS BUSINESS

A good friend at one of New York's most important modeling agencies gave me a piece of advice I'd like to pass on to you.

He said, "The girls who make it big are the ones who know how to treat it like a business. They know that being a model means being someone beautiful, someone special. But they know that there is more to life than that. They lead another life. When they're not working they act just like everybody else. They know that the world doesn't owe them anything just because they are pretty."

So accept your beauty as part of your business. Don't let it interfere with your personal life and don't be vain about it. It's tough, especially in the beginning, when a model has to accept more defeats than victories. But if you see it through you'll be well on your way to success.

MY FIRST YEAR

Enough philosophy for the moment. Let me tell you about my first year as a model. By the time I enrolled at the University of Toronto, thoughts of teaching gym (and being a ballerina) were behind me. I was studying Fine Arts and hoped to work in an art gallery or museum after graduation. Then I realized that I was very interested in design so I transferred to the Galasso School of Fashion Design and got my degree. After graduation I opened a boutique, Cykel 609, with two friends. We didn't make much money, but we had a lot of fun. We decorated the shop, bought as many clothes and accessories as we could and opened our doors for business. I even started designing "Viju Originals" which we made on a sewing machine borrowed from one girl's mother.

Being in the retail clothing business gave me an opportunity to see models in action. Every time I went to a manufacturer's showroom to buy clothes for our shop I saw models at work. And I mean work. Those girls changed clothes fifty times a day.

Since I was buying clothes as well as selling them, I got my first understanding of the psychology of fashion. If selling clothes depended only on the fact that people needed them, there would be no reason for fashion models. But because what we wear often expresses what we are, or think we are, or would like to be, putting clothes on a model helps the customer build an image.

I felt this would be helpful in our business, so my partners and I started "modeling" the clothes in our boutique. I loved it because I enjoyed coordinating dresses and shoes and accessories. Can you imagine having an unlimited wardrobe? Everything in the shop was at my disposal. I could wear anything I liked for a day and never have to wear it again. Fantastic!

Our shop got a lot of attention and one day a customer asked if we'd like pictures of us in the shop. She had a friend just getting started as a photographer and he wanted some experience in fashion photography. I said, "great," and a few days later he arrived.

FIRST JOB

Believe it or not, he actually did say, "Have you ever thought of becoming a model?" How many girls have heard that line? I said yes and went back to work.

14

He was serious, however, and before long he called to say that he had a job for me. At first I thought it was a joke but my friends persuaded me to give it a try and I did. My first job was posing for a brochure for an important chemical company. I think we were selling fertilizer. How's that for glamour?

If you think the rest was all champagne and *Harper's Bazaar*, forget it.

Although the chemical company loved the brochure, when I saw it, I went into shock. If I had had my way *nobody* would have seen it. Those pictures were quite a surprise. There I was. Too much hair. Too much makeup. I wanted to hide.

Finally, I taped the brochure photos to my bathroom mirror and forced myself to look at them every single morning. I now know that those photographs were probably the most helpful pictures I've ever had taken. Pictures like that show you what you are doing wrong. They give you a basis of comparison when you go to work to make it right.

Some people think that every shot a professional photographer takes must be good. If that were so, we'd all work about one hour a week. The fact is that a photographer takes hundreds of pictures and only a handful are usable.

Some are wrong because of technical reasons. In others, the model moved or the pose wasn't right. In still others, the model looks bad.

I felt I had looked awful in that brochure. That's why I started experimenting with different hairstyles and lighter makeup.

A TRADE SHOW

My next job was a little more encouraging, so I must have been doing something right. It was a trade show—the International Boat Show, in Chicago. Trade shows offer the most opportunities for models.

While at the boat show I greeted prospective customers, handed out brochures, talked to the visitors who stopped at our display and even tried to show people how the boats operated. Because my employer thought it would look "nautical," I wore a bikini. Convention halls tend to be large and drafty and I objected, but I learned another important lesson concerning modeling—the client is the boss. It probably helped to ward off a case of terminal goose bumps to remember that I was earning one hundred dollars a day.

The people at the show were super, especially the customers who listened to my sketchy explanations about the boats and then stayed long enough to explain the difference between port and starboard. Models who do these shows often know their products, but I, unfortunately, was a last minute choice and those patient weekend sailors kept me from making a fool of myself. Since then I've always had a warm spot in my heart (if nowhere else) for trade shows because that job really made me feel like a professional.

I wish I could say it also put me on the road to fame and fortune. Actually, I wish I could say that after the show I was steadily employed. Unfortunately, that was not the case. I was learning. I got a few jobs. And I was still making the kinds of mistakes that cost me jobs. I didn't have a good agency representing me at the time so most of the jobs I got were the result of marching through the doors of ad agencies, department stores and showrooms and asking for work. I still do.

Even with a good agency many models make the rounds on their own. And they get plenty of jobs that way. It is only those in constant demand who can afford to wait for the calls.

A good agency makes life easier because it sets up appointments for you where jobs are available. And they take care of your fees. But I'll explain all that later.

If I had to pick just one word to describe my first year as a model, I think it would be "exhausting." Since I couldn't work full time at the boutique I sold my share. My money went fast. Another lesson was learned that first year—how to budget.

Since my budget didn't cover taxifare all over Toronto, I took the bus. Or I walked. And walked. By the end of the average day I was usually so exhausted that I would take a quick shower and fall into bed without washing my hair or properly cleansing the makeup off my face. I thought I was being ambitious with all that running around. That was dumb. If a model arrives on the job looking tired and messy the client may fire her on the spot. Or call her agency and complain. That does nothing for her reputation.

16

SOME LESSONS LEARNED

Another few lessons learned. I started getting eight hours sleep each night. I washed my hair the day before it was needed, not the day after. I removed every spot of makeup each night no matter how tired I was. It finally paid off.

There was one mistake I didn't make, however, and I might as well tell you right now.

Without going into the grim details—I found myself at lunch with a man who said, in effect, "If you're nice to me, honey, I'll see to it that you get the job."

At that I picked up my portfolio and left. Sure, it happens. But not as often as some people like to think. As I've said, professional modeling is a multimillion dollar business. The really important people treat it that way. At the time I knew I was doing the "right thing," but looking back I know I also did the best thing for my career.

If you want to be a victim for every fast talking guy you meet nobody can stop you. But let me tell you the facts of life. As big as our business is, everybody knows everybody else. If a model starts playing games with the client or taking sleazy jobs, it's *her* reputation that goes down the drain. Ironically, the kind of guy who makes these offers couldn't get himself arrested, let alone get you a job. He's on his own ego trip, so don't let anyone kid you. Or con you. If you've got what it takes to get to the top of the profession, you'll get there by being the best model you know how to be and not because somebody offers you the "easy way." It's your looks and your reputation that count. Take care of both of them.

When I decided to do this book I thought about the reasons for it for a long time before I started writing. Anyone starting on a new venture should spend some time thinking about the reasons behind his or her actions.

That's why I'm going to ask you a very important question. Do you really know why you want to become a professional model? Is it an ego trip? Is it the glamour, the potential fame? Or maybe the money? Or is it a combination of all these? Whatever your reason I hope it's realistic, because it may be all you have to sustain you when you find yourself on an endless round of go-sees.

THINK IT THROUGH

Before you get out on a limb I suggest you do some serious thinking. Goals, like finishing high school, or maybe college, may seem insignificant now, especially if you're absolutely convinced you've got what it takes to be a top model. But remember, education lasts a lifetime and any decision affecting the rest of your life should be treated with great seriousness.

I've known a lot of girls who made the wrong decisions and would like a chance to do it differently. There are those girls who would like to give up and go back home, but their false sense of pride keeps getting in the way. It isn't much fun having to admit that you just didn't make it.

I've also heard the same stories you've probably heard about the girls who come to the big city to give "modeling a whirl" and, wouldn't you know, they're earning a hundred thousand dollars a year. Well, it can happen. But the few who reach that pinnacle are hardly the basis for a decision that may affect your whole life.

Fairy tales are for children but professional modeling is definitely for adults. I don't mean "adults" in the sense of chronological age. There are plenty of young girls who are tremendously successful models before they're old enough to vote. The number of years you've lived isn't nearly as important as how you've lived them. By that, I mean how you've dealt with your life so far. If you're a quitter, or a person who can't take competition or criticism, then success in this profession (or any other) may be beyond your grasp.

WHAT IT TAKES

However, if you think you've got what it takes, not just in looks, but in the qualities that really count, like a mature attitude towards work and a reserve of inner strength to see you through the rough beginnings, then you should do everything in your power to become a professional model.

18

This book may be a little different from what you might expect. Instead of taking a lot of space telling you how models do all the everyday things, I'd rather give you details of some really important aspects of modeling. Like how to get yourself together both physically and mentally so that when you go on your first interview you are fully prepared for whatever may happen.

If there is any secret in this business it's knowing who you are and what you want to do. Once you know that, then you can start preparing to achieve your goal. That's what this book is all about. I want to help you get where you want to go. I think it would be fantastic to meet a model one day who would say, "Viju, after I read your book I went out and got a modeling job and I still think that your book helped me get where I am today."

That's what I want. To help you become a successful model. So let's get started.

It's a good idea to check your measurements frequently. I do, at least once a week.

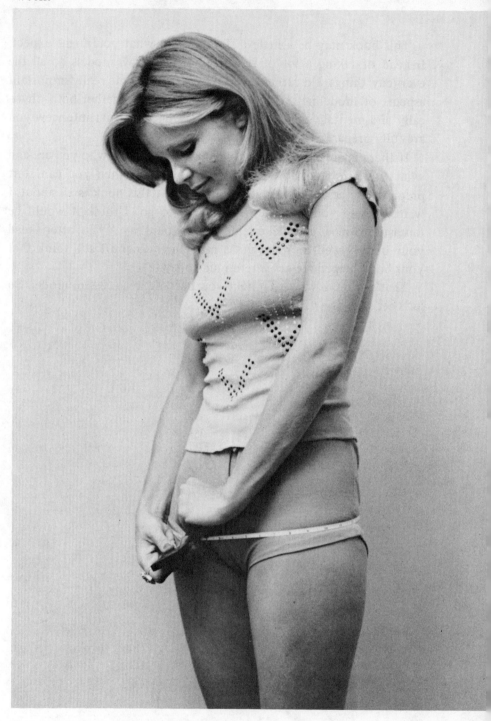

do you measure up?

Do you measure up? As a model, that is.

There are certain basic physical requirements for modeling that you should meet although there is a wide range within those requirements.

Few models are perfect or ideally beautiful in every respect. Unless, however, you are planning to become a character model (play a certain role such as an overweight teenager or middle-aged housewife), you should be well proportioned and at, or below, the normal weight for your height and bone structure.

Since there are different types of modeling jobs as you will see in the chapter on the various kinds of modeling, the same physical characteristics are not essential for all girls. The fashion model is tall (five-feet-seven and up) and willowy, with a very slim figure. Fashion models, however, don't have the so-called perfect figure looked for in beauty queens. They tend to have smaller busts and narrower hips. In other types of modeling, and even in some fashion work, a fuller figure is indicated. While the fashion model may have high cheekbones and a slim jawline, the rounder face of the girl-next-door look is often required for product advertising. And the beauty queen prototype is not as much in demand as she once may have been.

THE NATURAL LOOK

The "natural look" has become more important than ever. Lauren Hutton, probably the most successful model in the business these days, who, in 1974, signed a three-year exclusive $400,000 contract with Revlon, the cosmetics company, is not generally considered beautiful. She says of herself, "I have a space between my teeth and a ball on my nose. My face is lopsided."

Photographer Richard Avedon who has taken most of her photographs says, "She was the girl-next-door, but she moved away." And a New York newspaper that published a major article about her, headlined it, HUTTON: *The model who looks like a girl.*

It took time and hard work for Lauren Hutton to get where she is. When she started in 1967, several model agencies rejected her before Ford Models signed her. If there is any moral here, it is that persistence and confidence pays off. She certainly didn't look like many of the other successful models of the time.

ABOUT HEIGHT

Most models, in addition to being slender, are on the tall side. But Patsy Sullivan at five-feet-three didn't let her short stature stand in the way. She marched into Yardley of London, photos in hand, and was signed to do the Yardley Face Slicker ad campaign. While she knew she would never make it in the high fashion league, she did have a special look. And a major cosmetic company flipped over her. They were more interested in her face than in her height.

Bonnie Toman, another short girl, with the girl-next-door look, has been very successful at making television commercials for home products.

At the other end of the scale, Veruschka, one of the most famous high fashion models of our time, is six feet tall. So is Margaux Hemingway, a Wilhelmina model, who is being hailed as *the* model of the future (and present).

So, you see, you don't have to be a specific height although it is true that the majority of successful models are around five-feet-seven or five-feet-eight. But, as I've said, there are certain other physical requirements you'll have to meet.

22

Lauren Hutton, a Ford model, won a big contract with Charles Revson, Inc. representing Ultima II.

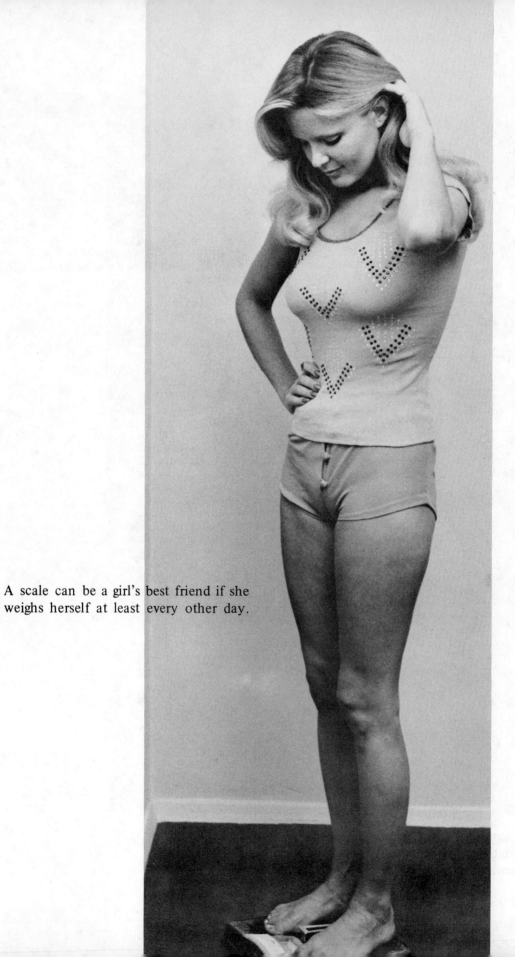

A scale can be a girl's best friend if she
weighs herself at least every other day.

How do you go about determining whether or not you do measure up as a potential model?

No doubt you have received assurances from friends and relatives that you are very pretty, and this has inclined you towards a career in modeling. You probably wouldn't be reading this book if you didn't have thoughts along this line.

LOOK AT YOURSELF

The first step is to take a good look at yourself from all angles. You might as well start with your figure, both in and out of clothes.

You will need a scale and a full length mirror. Preferably without your clothes, weigh yourself. Does your weight fall within the limits set on the chart provided on the next page?

This chart prepared by the Metropolitan Life Insurance Company is a good guide to what you should weigh. Girls who wish to model, however, should be in the lower end of the weight scale for their height and body frame. Most models are lighter than the chart indicates.

Generally speaking, whether you have a small, medium or large frame is determined by the size of your bones. Your hands, wrist, shoulders, ankles and general skeletal appearance will give you an idea of your body frame size. Girls who are definitely large boned or those who are small boned will know immediately their frame category. However, it is sometimes difficult to tell. You might have broad shoulders and narrow hips or vice-versa, although, I hope, not in an exaggerated way. Or you may have a small wrist and proportionately larger ankles.

You just have to make a judgment on the bone structure or frame category in which you belong. Your friends or your parents can be helpful also.

DO YOU LIKE WHAT YOU SEE

Now that you have determined your frame and weight, and while you still have your clothes off, look in the mirror. Do you like what you see?

The chart below gives desirable weights for girls and women for good health. Figures are given for age 18. Subtract one pound for each year under 18 down to age 15 and add one pound for each year up to age 25.

Height is your actual height without shoes. Weighing should be done without clothes.

Most models are about 5 to 10 pounds lighter than the lower end of the scale for their frame. For that reason they must be sure that their diet includes important nutrients *and* that they check frequently with their doctors to maintain good health.

Height	Small Frame	Medium Frame	Large Frame
5'	92–100	97–109	105–121
5'1"	95–103	100–112	108–124
5'2"	98–115	103–116	111–128
5'3"	101–109	106–120	115–132
5'4"	104–113	110–125	119–136
5'5"	108–117	114–129	123–140
5'6"	112–121	118–133	127–144
5'7"	116–125	122–137	131–148
5'8"	120–130	126–141	135–153
5'9"	124–134	130–145	137–156
5'10"	128–138	134–149	143–163

Over 5'10" add 2 to 4 pounds for every inch of height.

Please don't misunderstand me. No one is perfect. Many a successful model has some physical features she would prefer to see improved. But that is why you are looking at yourself. To find out if you approve of the shape *you* are in and also to determine if there is something you can do about it.

By that I mean—are you completely satisfied with what you see. Or, are your hips too full? Is there too much fat on your thighs? How is your posture? Do you stand tall, or do you slouch?

If you are too heavy, you will want to take off the excess weight by going on a diet. If there is excess fat on places such as your midriff, hips or thighs you will have to think about exercising it away.

Next, dress yourself and see how you look fully clothed. Check your appearance in dresses, both short and long; in slacks, in a sweater and skirt.

You should also check yourself from the back. Does your derriere bulge? This, too, can often be corrected by diet and exercise.

At any rate, no matter how pretty you are, before becoming serious about a modeling career, you should look your very best.

CLOTHING SIZES

If you are thinking about fashion modeling, or even if you are not, you should know something about the sizes of women's clothes and the size you are.

Women's clothes fall into two basic categories—Junior and Misses.

Juniors tend to be more slightly built with a shorter distance between shoulders and waist. Misses are more fully constructed with longer waists, fuller busts and slightly wider hips.

Junior sizes are the odd numbered sizes, 5-7-9-11, while Misses sizes are even numbered, 6-8-10-12. Depending on the general configuration of a model and because of adjustments that can be made for photographic purposes, she is often able to wear sizes in either category. So a model may list herself as available for sizes 5-6-7 or 6-7-8 or 7-8-9.

The height of women in the general population varies greatly, from under five feet to six feet and over. But for fashion modeling you shouldn't be shorter than five-feet-six. Most fashion models are five feet seven or eight while high fashion models are often taller. However, in showrooms and fashion show and runway modeling shorter girls may be needed if the manufacturer or merchant wants to show how his clothes look on a Junior Petite (women who are five feet two or shorter) or in some cases, on fuller figures. Obviously the top-notch fashion jobs go to models who are closest to the preferred taller heights.

Juniors are in big demand for modeling assignments for national magazines like *'Teen, Seventeen, Co-ed* and *New Ingenue* as well as *Mademoiselle* and *Glamour.* These monthly publications feature junior fashions and generally rely on agencies to supply their modeling needs. However, they also "discover" modeling talent. The 1973 Model of the Year, Linda Tongé, now a familiar face in Breck ads, as well as in fashion and beauty spreads in *Seventeen, 'Teen, Glamour,* and *Harper's Bazaar*, was discovered by the editors of *'Teen* when she entered a beauty contest through the magazine. Although a finalist in the pageant, she wasn't the winner. However, the editors liked her looks so much they kept using her in their editorial presentations. Linda, a small-town girl from Williams Bay, Wisconsin, who never dreamed all of these things would happen to her, is now a top model with Stewart Models in New York.

But back to *you.*

YOUR MAKEUP

In addition to wanting to put your figure in the best possible shape, you will also want to check your face and your makeup. Skillfully applied makeup can do just what it says—make up for some physical lack. If your skin is less than perfect it can be helped by the use of various cosmetics such as moisturizers or foundations. If you find that your present makeup is causing your skin to erupt, try the hypo-allergenic cosmetics that are on the market.

Are your eyebrows shaped in the best possible way for your face and eyes? If not, plan to do something about it.

Check out some of the beauty books or magazines that have articles on the subject. Or consult a knowledgeable friend or professional beautician.

28

And your hair? There is no doubt that certain hair styles look better on different individuals than other styles. What looks best on you? Are you at your best with long hair or short hair? Do you make a better appearance with straight hair or with it set in waves or in a specific hair fashion?

While it is true that some girls look just as appealing with any number of hairstyles, there is usually one which is preferred. You may look just as good with your hair long as you do with it short, but if you prefer it long and feel more comfortable and more attractive that way, wear it long.

As far as modeling goes, the development of wigs and other hairpieces has made it much easier for a girl to have her hair the way it is wanted for a particular assignment.

A STYLE OF YOUR OWN

You will want to develop a style of your own. Obviously, it should be the way you look your best.

The same goes for clothes. At one time models dressed only in the height of fashion when they went out in public. But that was some time ago. Now, many models may be seen trudging around New York or Los Angeles in jeans or slacks.

That should not prevent you from realizing that there are certain clothes in which you look best since there are times when that is the way you will want to look. And while you may wear blue jeans on the way to a modeling assignment, when you are working you'll have to wear all kinds of clothing, so you should have some idea of how you look in different outfits.

While clothing, hairstyles and accessories are very often specified by the client or photographer (depending upon the assignment), it doesn't hurt to know something about accessorizing clothes. I've often been able to add an attractive note to an outfit I'd be modeling since I know some of the things I look best in. While this may not always be welcomed, it still doesn't harm to learn some of the fundamentals of fashion and to apply them in your own dress.

Look through the current fashion and teenage magazines. Study the models pictured there and see if any have the kind of look you'd like to have or which resembles your own physical type. You might try the hairdo that one of them is wearing or see if you can duplicate her makeup. If you find one who seems to have the same color and shape eyes you have, try to see how close you can come to the shade of eye shadow or liner she is using.

If in doubt about the use of cosmetics or if you are not satisfied with the look you have with your present makeup, you might watch for the makeup clinics in department stores. Cosmetic companies frequently send experts to these stores who advise women on the proper makeup for their skin type and tone. While these specialists are there to help sell the cosmetic products, their advice could be helpful in enhancing your appearance.

Basically, that is what is involved in preparing yourself for a modeling career—learning how to enhance your appearance. Whether it be slimming down or making up, learning some pointers about fashion or how to stand and walk, you are preparing yourself.

As I said, confidence is an important characteristic to develop. To have confidence you must think well of yourself. And the better you look, the greater will be your self-esteem. I'm not talking about becoming vain. Or snobbish. Vanity and snobbishness can turn off a great many people who might be helpful to you in your career and in your life.

YOUR BEAUTY ROUTINE

Develop a beauty routine. As you will read in the chapter on A Day in the Life of a Model (mine), I have a regular evening beauty routine. I think almost every model has. It's a little like an athlete keeping in shape. Start keeping in shape now for those anticipated assignments.

Proper hair care is something you must always be aware of. The best looking hair is that which is healthy and clean. Frequent washings on a regular basis will meet both requirements. How frequently you wash your hair depends to some extent on where you live. In a city like New York which has a high degree of air pollution, a washing every other day is needed.

Daily, regular skin care is also vital. It is most important to keep your skin clean. Never go to sleep before you have cleansed away all the dirt and grime that gathers during the day. That also goes for any

ir care is an important part of your beauty
utine. Frequent washings and regular brush-
g coupled with proper nutrition will keep
ur hair clean and sparkling.

makeup you may have on. If you have a serious skin problem you should consult a dermatologist.

Plenty of rest is the mainstay of any beauty regimen. Lack of sleep produces puffy, lackluster eyes that have dark circles under them. And sparkling eyes can be the most alluring aspect of your facial look. Plan your life so that you get eight hours of sleep every night.

If you are thinking of changing your hair color, be very careful. The improper use of home hair coloring outfits and poor jobs by some professionals have brought grief to many a girl. If you do decide to change color, try on a wig of the color you want, to find out if the shade really looks good on you. But remember, the natural look is in, so your own natural hair color may be the best after all.

Don't forget to eat properly. Foods that are nutritious contribute to clear skin and shiny hair as well as to good general health. Empty calories (soft drinks, candy, cake, etc.) do nothing for you except add unwanted weight.

In other words, take care of yourself. While this is probably good advice for anyone, it is essential to a girl planning a career in model-ing.

facial care and makeup

FACIAL CLEANSERS
(Upper Left)
A vital step in beauty care is to be sure to remove all your makeup each night before getting your beauty sleep. Many models remove all their makeup right after a day's shooting and if they are going out for the evening they apply fresh cosmetics.

While soap and water make a very effective cleansing agent, you may find regular soap too harsh for your skin. There are many good cleansing creams and lotions on the market. Try a few to find the one that suits you.

ASTRINGENTS AND MOISTURIZERS
(Upper Right)
After you have used a facial cleanser to remove all your makeup, you should close your pores with an astringent and follow that by applying a moisturizer. A moisturizer does just what it says — it helps replace the skin's natural moisture removed during the cleansing process.

If you have a dry skin you may have to avoid astringents especially if they contain alcohol. And if any product you use causes irritation or redness don't use it.

BLUSHERS
(Lower Left)
A blusher will highlight and contour your cheeks and bring color to them much the way rouge does. Blushers can also help soften or strengthen other facial features such as chin and forehead. Blusher comes both in powder and cream form and should be applied with a light touch and carefully blended into your natural coloring.

LIPSTICK
(Lower Right)
Lipstick and lip gloss which some women have dispensed with in recent years is back in style. It is a must if you are being photographed and will always enhance your appearance. Fashions in lipstick colors change frequently and range from very pale to very deep tones. You'll want to experiment with several types to find the shades that go best with your own skin coloring.

kinds of modeling

To many people the concept of a model brings to mind the girl whose face graces the covers of magazines such as *Vogue, Harper's Bazaar, McCalls, The Ladies Home Journal* and countless other fashion and women's magazines. Or perhaps it is the girl displaying the latest fashions on the inside pages of the same publications.

Modeling, however, covers a far wider range of activities than this. In fact, the term model is often extended to areas somewhat remote from actual modeling. But be assured that there are many types of modeling and more opportunities in the field than you have even imagined.

MODELING CATEGORIES

I suppose all modeling could be divided into three basic categories with many sub-divisions. The three groups are photographic modeling, live modeling and television modeling.

Within the field of photographic modeling there are two main sub-categories—editorial and advertising. Editorial modeling involves photographs of all types that explain or enhance the text of the magazine or publication in which they appear. This category is also referred to as illustrative modeling. Advertising or commercial modeling is the kind appearing in ads bought in newspapers and magazines by a company to help sell a particular product. There are also other types of commercial modeling.

Redheaded model Darlene Camille is a slim 110 pounds at five-feet-seven and a half.

Kimiko Katayama came to the United States as the "Pearl of the Orient" promoting those precious jewels. She now has a permanent job modeling for a prominent Seventh Avenue dress firm with time off for TV commercials and photo assignments.

Rates of payment tend to be higher for advertising work and from this standpoint, more desirable. However, editorial or illustrative photographic modeling often carries with it a certain amount of prestige, especially if your picture appears on the cover of a national magazine or newspaper supplement.

FASHION MODELING

A large segment of photographic modeling, both editorial and advertising, is devoted to fashion. Fashion photography, in both groupings might well be called a category of its own as the fashion model must meet very specific physical requirements.

Perhaps the most familiar type and the aspect of fashion photography that gets the most attention, and also seems to be the most glamorous, is high fashion. This area is usually identified with magazines, primarily *Vogue* and *Harper's Bazaar*. They are published in the United States and also have editions in Great Britain, France, Italy and Australia. Then there are the other fashion magazines of France, Italy, Germany and other countries.

The high fashion model is a familiar physical type. The prototype of the high fashion model is the exceedingly slim girl with a small bust and narrow hips. Facially, she has high cheekbones and is almost always pictured practically without any expression. For years the high fashion publications have displayed the latest offerings of the world's leading designers on this type of model.

Only girls who were pencil slim and generally quite tall (five-feet-eight to six feet) would even be considered for this work. However, high fashion magazines are changing some of their concepts. Depending upon the kind of clothes or accessories being displayed, models with fuller figures and rounder faces now often grace the pages of these publications.

While high fashion modeling has always been the most glamorous of all types, it represents only a small percentage of overall fashion modeling. The financial backbone of the fashion industry is the lower and medium priced ready-to-wear lines. After all there is a limited market for gowns costing $500 and $1,000, designed by a Halston or Geoffrey Beene or any of the famous high fashion (or haute couture) designers.

That's why opportunities in fashion photography are so much greater in everyday clothing. For every ad that appears for an expensive garment, there are dozens, not to say hundreds, for those in the $15 to $150 range. This is true for dresses, suits, coats, sports and casual clothing, bathing suits, jewelry, accessories and lingerie. Just about every item a woman might need or wear.

Magazines such as *Glamour, Mademoiselle* and *Seventeen* devote a lot of editorial and advertising space to fashion. *Cosmopolitan* and *Teen*, as well as the general women's service magazines such as *McCall's* and *Ladies Home Journal* also devote space to fashion.

NEWSPAPERS

Then, of course, there is a vast amount of advertising and editorial coverage of fashion in daily newspapers. Department stores and specialty shops display their offerings on live models who are then photographed.

There are also services which send out news of the fashion world to these papers. While much of this photography is done in New York City, a certain amount is handled in the cities in which the stores are located.

CATALOGS

A very important segment of fashion modeling is done for the large catalog houses such as Sears Roebuck and Montgomery Ward. Thousands of photographs of all kinds of garments worn by models appear in these catalogs each year.

While a mail order catalog can't compete with *Vogue* or *Harper's Bazaar* and does not want to as far as exotic fashions or unusual layouts, catalog modeling is among the best paying of all modeling assignments. Earning fifty to sixty thousand dollars a year which is what some catalog models earn has a glamour of its own, not to mention solidity.

A good catalog model works constantly. Most companies put out two major catalogs a year and several supplements which feature fashion items.

You might think that a model who is something of a celebrity makes the most money in this business. Actually the opposite is

38

This ad for Kayser took me to Mexico
City.

often true. A model with Veruschka's distinctive looks is in demand for specific kinds of work but I doubt that she would be hired to model a ten dollar nightgown. Yet there are so many more opportunities in the lower priced garments and the amount of modeling it involves, that this area can bring in a large income.

Almost every department store of any size now has its own Christmas catalog. While many of the photographs which appear are duplicated in various other catalogs, this is still an area offering great opportunities.

Similar to catalog modeling is that which is done for the flyers and mailing pieces department stores and other retailers send out with their customer billings. There are a great many of these mailings made in every city each month. These, too, involve the displaying of all kinds of garments, usually in the lower and medium price ranges.

And let's not forget advertising and editorial appearances in the trade magazines that go to the manufacturers, wholesalers and retailers involved in women's wear businesses of all kinds. There is a lot of work here as well.

PRODUCT ADVERTISING

Another familiar type of photographic modeling is in the advertising of products other than fashion. This, too, can be divided into two kinds.

In one category the model is using the actual product. She may be driving a car, or consulting a dictionary, or eating a prepared food, or using a detergent. A wide range of feminine types is needed here.

A model using a household product need not be an outstanding beauty. Of course, she should have a pleasing appearance but the advertiser wants the potential customer to identify with the woman or girl in the ad. If the model were too breathtakingly beautiful, the reader might think, "That's not me." A different type of model might be sought for such a product than for a perfume or cigarette ad.

In the other type of product advertising the beauty of the model is used to attract the reader's attention (often a man) to the product. The product may be a camera or a stereo component, or a watch and the model may or may not be using or wearing the product.

40

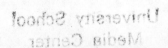

In still another situation the advertiser may want to create the illusion that his product (perfume, makeup, candles, etc.) will bring out the latent beauty and charm of any woman. Here beauty becomes a prime requisite.

EDITORIAL ILLUSTRATION

Another area of photographic modeling that involves various types of feminine appeal is the editorial photo that supplements a story in a magazine. It may be fiction or it may be an article dealing with some psychological or social aspect of life.

A cover appearance celebrating the 100th anniversary of the Canadian Northwest Mounted Police.

Cosmopolitan, one of the most successful magazines of current times, frequently uses posed photographs to depict life situations between men and women.

In perhaps a less prestigious way, confession, crime and true life story magazines use live models in dramatic photographs to illustrate their stories.

A fashion model displays a Bill Blass design as buyers take notes.

PUBLICITY AND PUBLIC RELATIONS

Models are frequently used to dress up or call attention to a product or festival or other event. A girl may pose for photographs as she opens a real estate subdivision or selects the first fresh fruit of the season. Such photographs are sent to newspapers and wire services to help in the promotion of the event or product. A pretty girl still seems to be the best way to attract many an editor's eye. In the same way models are used to call attention to the opening of a fair or bazaar or celebration.

LIVE MODELING

The most important area of live modeling is the fashion world. Clothing—sportswear, evening dress, dresses and suits are displayed on the model, most usually to a prospective buyer. The latest collection of a renowned designer may be unveiled at a press event.

Modeling clothes in person is very basic to the profession of modeling as that is where the whole thing started. To this day there is still no better way to show how a garment looks than to present it on a live model.

There are fashion shows *and* fashion shows. The most important fashion showings occur when designers present their latest creations. This happens at stated times during the year and fashion editors from all over the world converge on Paris, Rome or New York to gather information about the "new looks."

Of course, the models who present the creations of leading designers have to be very skillful since, in one sense, the eyes of the whole world are on them. Many such models work exclusively for one designer and present his or her clothes to customers at other times during the year. Such permanent jobs for top designers however, are few in number. Many other models who specialize in fashion work are called upon only for special occasions. Live fashion modeling is often referred to as runway modeling since the girls presenting the clothes parade up and back on a raised wooden walk, much like a stage, to enable the audience to get a better view of the garments.

Twice during each year a Press Week is designated in New York and fashion editors and reporters from all over the United States arrive to be shown the latest offerings at breakfasts, lunches, dinners and in-between events. Many major companies which produce fabrics—companies like DuPont, Celanese and others require fashion models. These events are usually held at one or another of the major New York hotels like the Waldorf-Astoria, the Americana, the Plaza and others.

Then there are several Market Weeks when buyers arrive upon the Seventh Avenue scene (New York's wholesale clothing market) to view the latest collections of major fashion houses. At other times of the year the new season's presentations are also brought forth. These are hectic times indeed for the live fashion model. It is D-Day, the Fourth of July and New Year's Eve all rolled up into one incredible week-long fashion show.

Sometimes a model is called upon to show more than two dozen outfits within an hour. The buyers sit in the showroom, notebook ready, pencils poised. Each model does her best to show off every aspect of the outfit she is wearing. She introduces each outfit by number. If the buyer likes it he starts jotting down the numbers. You can feel the tension in the air. If the buyers don't like the new line, a manufacturer can find himself in serious financial trouble. If they do like it, it's time to celebrate.

Meanwhile, back in the dressing rooms things are really frantic. These rooms, meant to accommodate two or three models at a time, are shared by as many as five or six. The lighting may not be good and a place in front of the one available mirror isn't easy to get. Aren't you glad you have a folding mirror in your tote? "Who's wearing number 135? Who's got my left shoe? Has anybody seen my barrette?" And so it goes.

The live fashion show is still one of the best places for a would-be model to learn her trade. And it is one of the best places for a professional model to pick up extra money.

MODELING FOR WHOLESALERS

Many live fashion modeling jobs are available on New York's Seventh Avenue, the world renowned wholesale garment district. Here several thousand companies engaged in manufacturing and sell-

44

ing women's clothes of all types and at all prices, occupy the buildings ranged along Seventh Avenue from 30th to 40th Streets and beyond and on the side streets which cross the avenue.

Almost all of these companies use models to show their wares to buyers from department stores and specialty shops who turn up in New York at various times of the year looking for new merchandise. But modeling for a wholesale dress house or a manufacturer or distributor of women's fashions usually includes other business chores and general office work as well. A few of the larger houses employ full time models who do nothing but model. But the average garment manufacturer who has a need for a model perhaps only 10% or 20% of the time employs a girl who does double duty.

Most often these wholesale fashion houses will be looking for models in specific sizes such as 7-9 or 10-12 to model the kind of clothes they produce. This may be Junior sizes or Misses or even for more matronly figures. Such jobs are often advertised in the Help Wanted section of *The New York Times. Women's Wear Daily*, the newspaper devoted to the women's fashion field, also carries advertising for showroom models as well as providing a lot of valuable information about all aspects of the industry.

Such houses are interested principally in a girl with a good figure who can show off their clothes. Such jobs don't pay much more than other clerical or secretarial jobs which means about $130 to $175 per week. However, this field can provide good modeling experience.

RETAIL MODELING

Then there is the presentation of fashions in the retail area. Various department stores and major specialty shops use models at different times, either in a formal fashion show or to walk through the department so that customers will see how the latest fashions look when worn.

Many charitable and civic organizations have fund raising lunches and dinners at which a fashion show is part of the entertainment. While such events often have the services of celebrity models (actresses or socially prominent women) they also usually need a few professional models.

Christine Busini, represented by the Filor Agency, was chosen to be New York City's 1975 Summer Ambassador.

CONVENTION AND TRADE SHOWS

Another extensive area of live modeling opportunities is the convention and trade show field. Remember I told you that a job at a boat show was one of my first modeling assignments.

At trade shows and at some business conventions manufacturers of all kinds of products show their wares to prospective buyers—usually retailers who buy for resale to the public. Sometimes the trade shows are open to, or held for, the general public. Each manufacturer or distributor has a booth and very often will want one or more models to be present, both to attract visitors and answer questions.

While this work is not as exciting or glamorous as a fashion show or posing for photographs, it can often provide valuable experience in meeting the public and in developing poise and confidence. And it can provide a reasonably good income and doesn't take all your time. While the rates for this work vary widely, it is not unusual for a model to get $150 a day or more while manning a booth at a trade show. The shows extend from several days to a week.

Certain agencies specialize in providing models for conventions and trade shows. Some girls are particularly adept in dealing with the public and are in demand for many of these events.

GOODWILL AMBASSADORS

Just as in the photographic field, there are also good opportunities for models to become festival queens or the goodwill ambassadors for products. Only instead of being a one day matter, the job may continue for the better part of a year.

New York City chooses a Summer Festival Queen, recently renamed Summer Festival Ambassador, from among models submitted by the various model agencies. This lucky girl gets to travel all over the United States and to Europe and South America as part of the program to publicize New York City as a great summer tourist attraction. She also participates in many events in the city and, of course, is paid very well.

While becoming Miss Peach Melba for an ice cream association or some similar designation may not be as interesting or as lucrative as being New York's Summer Festival Ambassador, there is a substantial call for models (who must possess outstanding personalities as well) for the festival and product promotion field.

TELEVISION

With the growth of television as a major entertainment and educational force, opportunities for modeling in this area grew along with it. Who is not familiar with the TV commercial in which products of all kinds are sold to the public? The list is long and varied. Soaps, toothpaste, perfume, toys, games, clothing, automobiles, packaged foods—it's almost endless. And most of these commercials use models of all kinds.

TV commercials provide a very lucrative income for the model but they also require more extensive talents than other types of modeling. A model doing a TV commercial is more akin to an actress. In fact many actresses who may, or may not, have been models have entered this field. Unlike still photography, the model presenting the product on TV must move well and her changing facial expressions must be pleasing. Often she is required to speak. These elements bring in a whole variety of talents.

Since TV commercials are so financially rewarding many models who have not had previous training, study acting and voice. Interestingly enough, some models who were successful at still photography moved into the motion picture field in this way.

TV commercials and other modeling assignments have been the jumping off place for important careers in motion pictures or television for a number of girls. Among them are Barbara Feldon, who went from doing perfume, deodorant and automobile commercials to a leading role in TV's long running "Get Smart" series; Lauren Hutton, who has appeared in half a dozen films: Cybill Shepherd, who has starred in "Daisy Miller," "The Last Picture Show," and other films; and Lois Chiles who played in "The Great Gatsby."

One of the reasons that television work is so financially rewarding is because if the commercial you've made is successful (it has helped substantially to sell the product) you will be paid not once but for each time the commercial is aired on TV and it can be shown many times. These payments which are called residuals can continue for years.

48

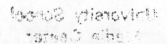

Charlie Hansen has made several movies
and enjoys a successful modeling career
as well.

Joan Westberg combines theatrical roles,
including musicals, with modeling assignments.

One girl I know collected more than $50,000 in two years for a commercial that took less than one day's time to make. Of course, an amount that large is not usual but many a girl has continued to reap benefits from a few hours' work over many months or more. The range is wide. You can earn from $5,000 to $20,000 for a successful commercial.

There is a whole schedule of payments based upon first use of the commercial and subsequent uses and the number of times used but I won't try to give it to you here.

GETTING INTO TV

If you are selected to make a TV commercial you must become a member of one or both of the two unions that represent television actors and performers. If you haven't heard these initials before you will as soon as you get involved in TV work—AFTRA (American Federation of Radio and Television Artists) and SAG (Screen Actors' Guild). You'll have to join one or both. AFTRA's jurisdiction is in the area of video tape while SAG's is film. Since commercials are taped and filmed, and you may be doing both types, this membership is necessary. The initiation fee for joining the first union is $300 and when you join the sister union it is half of that or an additional $150. In addition there are annual dues which vary according to your earnings and each union's regulations, but start at $40 to $50 per year and go up based on your annual TV earnings.

Just how does one go about getting into the TV commercial field? While the number of opportunities are not limitless the types of personalities are very broad indeed. It seems that all those involved, chiefly advertising agencies, are always searching for someone different or someone who fills a certain role.

Since advertising agencies are the principal purchasers of the air time on which TV commercials appear (as they are of magazine and newspaper space) a would-be TV model should make the rounds of the ad agencies. If the casting director likes your pictures an appointment will be set up. Don't expect to be given a lot of time at this interview but you might just have the characteristics a particular agency is looking for.

50

The cameraman is giving some instructions for the filming of a TV commercial.

The ad agencies do keep your photographs and composites on file for future use so if you don't make the rounds, you can't expect them to think of you.

TV Guide cites the estimate that about 2500 girls are involved in doing television commercials.

SPECIALITIES

There are a few other areas of live modeling such as posing for an artist or illustrator but more and more the drawings are sketched from photographs.

I should tell you a bit about specialty work for photography or TV. Certain models who have exceptional legs or hands are used to pose for ads showing those parts of their body only. A girl with terrific legs can do very well indeed posing for pantyhose or shoe ads. However, it is a somewhat limited field. But if you do have some outstanding physical characteristic it certainly doesn't hurt to try to get work in that area. And it doesn't prevent you from taking other jobs as well.

Sometimes a particular model is selected to represent a product on a long term basis. She becomes a semi-permanent promotion representative for that product and will appear in ads in newspapers and magazines, in television commercials, on window or in-store posters and will often make personal appearances. Her face will be seen everywhere, closely associated with the cosmetic or perfume or clothes she is helping sell. In that case she will most likely sign a contract for a specific period of time such as one, two or three years. Movie actress Catherine Deneuve has been representing Chanel No. 5 perfume for several years. Lauren Hutton has become the image of Charles Revson's Ultima II.

When a model or actress does sign a long-term contract to represent one company she cannot, of course, work for any competing product and, often is completely tied to that one organization. Even is she isn't, other clients may feel she is not suitable for them because an image has been established in the mind of the public and the client will turn to someone else. This is not always so.

52

Kay Sutton York, a Ford model, combines a
stage career with modeling. She has been seen
in ads for Max Factor cosmetics.

Gary Bernstein

Gunilla Knutson who gained renown as the "Take It Off" girl for Noxzema Shaving Cream has been a busy model since she arrived in the United States as Miss Sweden.

Gunilla Knutson who arrived in the United States as Miss Sweden in the Miss Universe contest took up a very successful modeling career. She first caught the public eye when she was selected to do television commercials for Noxzema Shave Cream. Her now famous lines, "Take it off, take it all off" and other promotional activities for that company identified her closely with the shaving cream. Since that time, however, she has done modeling and product promotion for many other different types of merchandise.

At any rate, I hope I've given you a good idea of all the areas of modeling which might open up for you once you get in the field. Sometimes a girl gets typed and remains in one branch of the profession doing only fashion or being a homebody type for detergents, but more usually a model who is in demand may do fashion work, pose for product advertising and do TV commercials as well. If a client likes your looks and the way you photograph it doesn't matter what your last assignment was.

Remember that advertisers and photographers are always on the lookout for a new face. It may be yours.

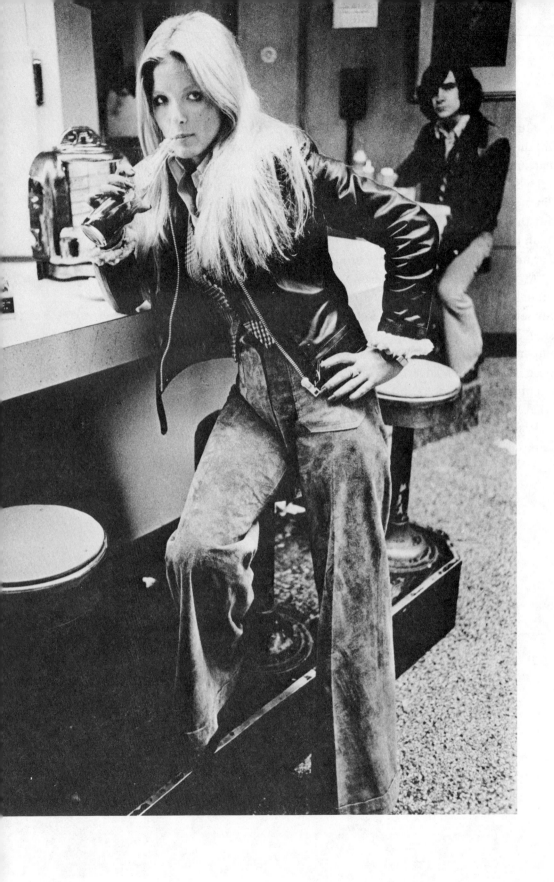

getting a job as a model

Now that we've talked about getting ready to be a model, I think the time has come to talk about actually becoming a pro. Naturally the question uppermost in the mind of every would-be model is "How do I go about getting a *real* modeling job?" I guess that's why so many girls ask me who to see, what to say, what to do and how to act when they start going out on interviews.

Surprisingly enough, some girls still cling to the notion that there is a secret way, a magic formula that will propel them into successful careers. The truth is that there is nothing "magical" about it. I would venture to say that any girl with the right qualifications who is in the right place, at the right time, will be able to get some professional modeling assignments. But if you are like most girls, you probably aren't interested in getting only a few assignments. A couple of fashion shows and a few pictures in a magazine don't add up to a successful modeling career. And since you want your career to be the biggest and best it can be I think the time has come to get down to the nitty-gritty of professional modeling.

As in any career, the girl who wants to become a professional model doesn't usually start at the top. There have been a few notable exceptions, girls who have been so spectacular looking that they are in demand right from the start. It is important for any would-be model to realize that this is the exception and not the rule. It takes a lot of hard work and often a lot of time before a really successful career can be launched. So don't get discouraged if you don't start out with a bang. Try to remember, just getting work as a professional model means that you've got something that most girls don't have.

The majority of successful, professional models are affiliated with one or another of the model agencies and I'll be telling you more about agencies in the next chapter. There are, however, some models who free lance and get jobs completely on their own, but having an agency represent you is by far the best way.

Therefore, after you have prepared yourself you will want to try to arrange an interview with one or more model agencies.

The largest and most important model agencies are in New York followed by Los Angeles and Chicago. New York, of course, is the center of modeling activity but many other cities have agencies. Montreal is the leading city for models in Canada.

That initial interview with an agency can be very important which is why I am devoting quite a lot of space to discussing various aspects of the interview.

Getting started in this business isn't very different from getting started in any new venture. First, you have to prepare yourself and when you think you're ready, you have to go out and try to convince the rest of the world that you've got what it takes.

THAT IMPORTANT INTERVIEW

In that sense, all job interviews are basically the same. Naturally, you want to put your best foot forward. And like most people, you are probably going to feel a little nervous and maybe even a little scared. When you decide to start being interviewed for modeling jobs these feelings are to be expected.

As I've said, professional modeling is a business and as such there

are people to see and procedures to follow just as there are in trying to get any other kind of job. Start thinking about your modeling career as an entry into the business world. That way you will have a basic frame of reference. I realize more and more that one should think that way especially when I hear stories like the one a friend who interviews girls for one of New York's top agencies told me recently.

This man has been in the industry for over twenty years so he has seen just about everything, but he was really amused and amazed by a girl who had appeared at his office the day before. Apparently she had decided that her "image" was one of chic sophistication and she was doing her level best to convince him that she really knew her way around.

"I don't know who she thought she was kidding," he said. "She looked like a kid wearing her mother's clothes and she acted like a road-company Salome. She was only fifteen years old!"

Needless to say, he was not impressed. Nobody would dress and act this way on any other job interview but some girls still think modeling is "different."

THE UNDERSTANDING INTERVIEWER

Since I know how nervous a girl can be on her first interview (or her twentieth for that matter) I asked him if people at the agencies were aware of the strain a girl may be under. "After all," I said, "just going on an interview at an important agency can be pretty scary. And don't forget, it's hard for a lot of girls to try to get a job based on their looks alone. That's a lot different from getting a job doing something that you can learn how to do."

He agreed completely. "Of course, agency people know a girl is going to be nervous. It's to be expected. That's why we try to put them at ease. And don't forget, we are basically interested in their looks on an initial interview. If they've got the 'look' we like, we don't worry too much about anything else. Hopefully, when they start working, they will learn to relax. But we have to rely on first impressions. So if a new girl is a little nervous, we discount it."

59

WHAT TO WEAR

I think the statement that we're basically interested in their looks, is crucial. We've already talked about developing a personal style but at the risk of sounding repetitive, let me emphasize the importance of looking your best on every interview. That means looking the way you would like to look when you actually start modeling. I don't mean that you should go out and spend a fortune on clothes you think a model would wear. Remember, today, models wear what they please. And what they wear is usually very low key and very stylish. So don't get decked out like a walking Christmas tree and please don't try to dress the part of a model based on some concept you may have developed. If you do you will probably be way off base.

If you are a teenage girl, dress like one. If you are a little older, don't dress like a little girl but on the other hand, don't dress like an old lady either.

THE PROPER LOOK

Use your head. And your mirror. If you have an outfit in your closet that has always looked good on you, wear it. Don't worry about the fact that it isn't brand new. If it makes you look good and *feel* good, you will have more confidence in your appearance than you would if you wear something new but aren't sure of.

Don't wear a lot of jewelry and accessories. If you come rattling and clanking to an interview, weighted down under a mass of necklaces, bracelets, earrings, belts and the Lord only knows what else, you are probably overdoing it. More important, the agency wants to get a good look at you. They want to be able to see your figure, your bone structure, your shoulders, your waist. Wearing a lot of glitter obscures your body and defeats your purpose.

Don't go in the opposite direction and show up in a skintight dress or pants suit. It isn't necessary and you will look just awful. Try to strike a happy medium. Pants are OK if they fit properly. But make sure that your tops aren't loose and flowing. A good pair of slacks will show the line of your leg and hip but an overblouse will obscure your waistline and cover your upper arm. Stick to fitted tops, tailored blouses and clingy sweaters.

Once you have selected a flattering outfit, wear it and stop thinking about it. You can't fuss with your clothes while you are being interviewed. Which is another reason I like to wear something familiar. If I've already worn an outfit, I know how it feels. It becomes part of me. I know it's comfortable and I don't have to worry about it being too loose or too tight. I've had time to get used to it and to have any necessary alterations made. Then I can concentrate on the real reason I am there—to get the job.

CHECK YOUR HAIR AND MAKEUP

The same holds true for your hair and makeup. Don't decide to try out a new hairdo the day of the interview. You're much better off wearing your hair in a familiar style. Since you're used to arranging it, you can get it to look its best with a minimum amount of fuss. And if you've been wearing it a certain way for a while, chances are it looks good. So why make a drastic change? If your hair is long, wear it down. If you are asked, you can always scoop it up so the agency interviewer can get a good look at your neck. Why take a chance of having a carefully arranged hairdo blown apart by the wind or rain? Simple styles are more easily corrected if something goes wrong on the way to the interview.

As for makeup, the less you wear, the better. Or perhaps I should say, the less that *shows* the better. The agency wants to see *you*. If you've been practicing and experimenting with makeup, by now you should be able to apply it in such a way that you look absolutely terrific and perfectly natural. Remember, these people know all the tricks. So you can't really fool them. If you normally wear lots of eye makeup and feel naked without it, by all means wear it. But don't be surprised if they ask if you always wear so much. On the other hand, if you don't usually wear a lot, don't pile on the paint because you think it's expected. Just try to look your prettiest. You'll feel a lot better if you stick with a look you know.

WHERE TO GO

OK, you're all ready to go. But go where? That's the real question at hand. Depending on what you've decided to do—either pursue a modeling career in your own hometown or try your luck in the big city—you have to get a job. So naturally you need a place to start.

There is a list of agencies in various cities in this book but to make sure that they are still there at a time like this a girl's best friend is the classified telephone directory. Sit down and make a list of modeling agencies (complete with phone numbers) and then pick up the phone and start calling. Believe it or not, many agencies will see new applicants just as soon as they can set up an appointment. Of course, the top agencies are awfully busy and probably won't be able to see you right away but the sooner you call for an appointment, the sooner you will get your interview. Agencies differ in their requirements but the receptionist will tell you what you need to know.

One top agency in New York interviews new applicants every morning between 9:30 and 10:00 am. Their receptionist is instructed to tell each caller that she is perfectly welcome to set up an appointment and come by for an interview just as long as she is at least five feet, seven inches tall. That's all they ask. That you be tall enough to suit their program and that you have the courtesy to make an appointment first before dropping in.

PHOTOGRAPHS

Since a lot of agencies do ask for a photograph before they decide to see an applicant, a lot of girls feel that they have to spend money on "professional" photos. Not so. If you've never had any modeling experience before (local fashion shows or beauty contests and the like) chances are you don't have any photographs other than your class pictures. While they make nice gifts for friends and relatives they really won't "send" a modeling agency.

But don't panic. You don't have to spend a lot of money. Have a friend, or someone in your family who is a camera buff, take some pictures. Most agencies want at least one head shot so they can get a good look at your face and one full length picture of you wearing something that shows your figure. These don't have to be professional photographs and they don't have to be "staged." If a friend

62

shoots a few rolls of film you can't help but get a couple of pictures that really look like you.

When it comes to the full length shots, the agency wants to see the same things they would want to see if you were there in person. That means a picture of you in a bathing suit or a sleeveless top and cutoffs will be more helpful than pictures of you on your way to a dance. They are interested in your shoulders, your upper arms, your waist, hips, thighs—your overall figure. They can tell by looking if you have the kind of frame a model needs to wear clothes well.

I asked an agency executive about professional photographs and he assured me that they were not necessary. "After all," he said, "if we like her, we know plenty of photographers who will take pictures of her. We will help her put her portfolio together and believe me, we know a lot more about the kinds of pictures she will need than people outside the business."

Of course, if you have a friend who is a professional photographer or know one who is willing to take your picture at no, or little expense, to you, it won't hurt. Just remember, it is not necessary to spend a lot of money on a professional photograph job.

So hold off on lots of pictures unless you can get them through local sources or from previous jobs. Once you start modeling you will meet photographers who will be happy to use you for test shots and provide free pictures in return for your time. Once you start working, you will have plenty of pictures to include in your portfolio. So don't try to get everything together before the interview.

If you've had some previous modeling experience and do have pictures, by all means bring them along—if they're good. If they aren't, don't bother. Some models are so entranced by any photograph of themselves that they can't resist showing it. But in this case a bad picture is *not* better than no picture at all. Remember the case of the model who wailed, "But I don't *always* look that way." If she had any sense at all she would never have asked for pictures of herself looking anything less than terrific.

The whole point of being a professional model is looking good in photographs. So why confuse the issue? The agency isn't interested in your long, sad story about the terrible cold you had the day these pictures were taken or how the photographer had trouble with his equipment or whatever excuse you've dreamed up. All they know is that you are dumb enough to bring *them* bad pictures which means that you just might not really care about what you are doing. That doesn't enhance your image with the agency one tiny bit.

DON'T COP OUT

Neither does copping out at the last minute. I mean by not showing up for your appointment. It may sound silly but I've heard of more than one girl who panicked at the thought of *actually going* on the very interview she had been dying to get just a week before. If something really serious prevents you from making your appointment, call and cancel it immediately. Give a reasonable explanation of why you won't be able to make it and ask for another appointment just as soon as possible.

If you are just suffering from a bad case of butterflies, keep the appointment. You aren't the first nervous applicant the agency has ever seen and you won't be the last. Don't decide to wait until some distant day when you feel "ready." Chances are you won't want to go then either. Let's face it. A model's life is composed of an endless round of interviews so if you want to be a professional model, the sooner you get started the quicker you'll get used to it.

Of course, if you start worrying about your interview you'll probably work up a real case of nerves. Instead of worrying about the things that might go wrong, start working on ways to make things go as smoothly as possible. If you adopt a businesslike manner ("businesslike," not phony sophistication) you will naturally make a better impression. Remember, this is potentially a job interview too. The agency is in a position to start you on your way to a successful career. You owe it to yourself and to them to have all the information necessary at your fingertips.

A FEW KEY POINTERS

For example, if you have just arrived from another city and you're staying with a friend or at a hotel, you probably don't have your new address and telephone number committed to memory. Write it down

64

in a notebook. If you move, let them know. If they decide they want to talk to you again you certainly don't want to miss their call.

Obviously, they will want to know your name, so make sure you give them your real name. Lots of girls decide to model under names they like better than the one their parents gave them but the agency needs your legal name.

Tell them your exact age because if you are still a minor your parents' or guardian's consent is necessary in signing legal documents. In most states a girl under eighteen is a minor in the eyes of the law. So be honest. The agency doesn't care how young you are as long as you've got what it takes. They *do* care about the law and they can get in a lot of trouble if you mislead them.

Answer all questions openly and honestly. They are being asked for good reason and the more efficiently you answer, the better impression you will give. Don't try to be "cute" or "sophisticated" for the agency's benefit. Tell them what experience you have had. But don't exaggerate. Some girls think agencies prefer models with lots of experience to a newcomer. This isn't the case at all. Agencies are always looking for a new face and a new look. So youth and lack of exposure are actually working for you.

INTERVIEW TIME

Often an interview with an agency representative may seem abrupt. I can sympathize with both sides. On one hand I know from experience how much these interviews mean to a would-be model. Hopes are high and you want desperately to make a good impression. But I also understand the agency's problem. It is an awfully busy place. Only a small part of the day can be spent answering letters and phone calls from new girls. When they do see you, the interview has to be brief. They want to see as many girls as possible in the time allowed. As experts, agency people can tell more about your modeling potential in ten minutes than you might expect. As business people, they can't take the time to be concerned about your ego. So be prepared for a brief interview. And when it's over don't try to prolong it. Leave the way you came—with style.

CHECK IT OUT

One of the most difficult aspects of interviews is knowing something about the agency beforehand. In New York, agencies like Ford Models, Wilhelmina Models and Stewart Models as well as some others are prestigious and there is no question as to their fine reputation. But there are many agencies all over the country and some, unfortunately, aren't so reputable. How is a girl to know what she's getting into before she arrives?

My favorite story about finding out about an agency beforehand has to do with a young girl from Oregon who had been told time and time again that she should be a model. When her family came East to visit she decided to spend a couple of days in New York making the rounds. She called one of the leading model agencies and was given an appointment. The day before the appointment she traveled to the agency to get her bearings. She had two reasons. Being unfamiliar with New York she wanted a test run on the subway. She also wanted to get a look at the agency's office building and the kind of neighborhood it was in before she went on the actual interview.

That is my idea of a smart girl. Not only did she plan to be sure that she knew how to get there, and on time, she also wanted to be certain that she *wanted* to be there. Since the agency was located in a perfectly respectable looking office building in a good area she decided to go in and take a look around. She was in the reception area when the agency director happened to come out of her office. The girl from Oregon impressed the director so much that she was given an interview then and there. Not having expected to see anyone, she protested that she would be happy to wait until the next day and didn't want to cause a fuss. But they liked her looks and her attitude. Today she is doing very well as a top model.

I'm not saying that you should just drop in on agencies. I do think it is a good idea to look them over and even ask about them. And if you don't know your way around it doesn't hurt to try a test run. If the agency looks cheap and disreputable, maybe you should think twice about keeping your appointment at all. (But do remember to cancel it.) There are still some pretty creepy outfits operating under the guise of "modeling agencies" so you'll have to learn to take care of yourself.

66

IN GOOD TASTE

Remember, a good agency will never ask one of its models to do any kind of modeling that isn't in good taste. The agency has its own reputation to protect. If for some reason you find yourself being asked to do something you don't think is right just excuse yourself and leave. Unfortunately, no one can make these decisions for you. No one can decide what's right and what isn't for you. That's why a would-be model needs that inner strength and maturity I was talking about. Learn to rely on your own good judgment and I don't think you'll ever regret it.

Cybill Shepherd started as a model and continues her work in the field but she has also starred in several outstanding movies.

the model agency

Those first model agency interviews are so all-important because the model agency plays a big role in the entire business of modeling. Most modeling jobs are booked through agencies, so it is highly desirable for you to be with one.

I, and most people, refer to firms that represent models as being model agencies. In some places, particularly New York State, a number of agencies are not technically employment agencies under the law which licenses such businesses since they perform functions other than just being an intermediary between the model and the client. They have taken the word agency out of their company name. However, all of them continue to be generally known as agencies and I'll be referring to them in that way.

Usually a girl will sign an exclusive contract with one agency. This contract empowers the agency to negotiate various financial arrangements on her behalf, arrange bookings, set and collect fees and generally handle any business dealings she may be involved in as a model.

The model agency also acts in other ways to help a young model make her way. When it has decided to take you under its wing, your picture, name and pertinent information is included in the "head-sheet" which is sent to clients and prospective clients. They will also distribute your composite. (More about that later.) You become identified with the agency and are known as a Wilhelmina model or a Ford model or a Stewart model in New York, or a Blanchard model in Los Angeles. When you are with a prominent agency it gives you a more important position in the world of advertising, publicity and product promotion. Even if your agency is not one of the leaders, the identification and the services it renders are very valuable. Even so, it is not impossible to make it on your own if you have the energy and desire.

AGENCY SERVICES

Chief among the agency's services to its models is the responsibility for collecting their fees. In years past a model would do a job for a client and then have to wait days, weeks or even months before she saw her check in payment. This proved disastrous to many girls who found themselves with a stack of unpaid bills and only a promise of payment for work done. And valuable time and energy are wasted when a model goes through the difficult procedure of collecting fees from a client who is slow in paying.

Even better, when a model does a job, she carries a voucher book which is signed by the client or photographer at the conclusion of the job. It becomes the official record of the number of hours she has worked and the amount of money she is owed.

FINANCES

When she turns over the signed voucher to her agency they will pay her a certain amount even before collecting her fee from the client. The payment is broken down in this manner by at least one agency. It takes 15% of the fee for its services. It then pays the model up to 70% of the remaining amount. The other 30% goes into what is generally called a "reserve fund." This becomes available to the model as soon as the agency collects the fee. Most agencies follow a plan similar to this.

Many girls use this reserve fund as a kind of bank account—allowing a substantial sum of money to accumulate so that they can draw upon it in case of emergency or if they decide to stop working for a while and take a vacation. Since many models don't work as often as they might like, learning to budget money is essential. Some models will earn a great deal of money in a very short period of time. Like anyone else with a large earning capacity, a model needs someone to advise her in financial matters. Many successful models get a business manager. Generally speaking the agency has nothing to do with how a model spends or invests her own money. By the terms of the contract they are obligated to collect her fees, withhold their commission and pay her on the prescribed basis. If a model wants financial advice, she should get a specialist in that field.

RELATIONSHIP WITH YOUR AGENCY

A model's relationship with her agency is very important to both of them. After signing an exclusive contract every modeling job (whether the agency gets the booking or the model gets it herself) comes under the terms of the contract. Having signed the agreement in good faith, no reputable model ever does a modeling job without telling her agency about it. The agency is legally entitled to a percentage of the income from all jobs no matter how the model gets them. Honesty is the best policy. The girl who may try to withhold knowledge of an assignment from her agency may find herself looking for someone else to represent her. If she earns a reputation for being dishonest, most good agencies won't want her. It would be foolish to jeopardize access to future work for very little.

The agency has certain responsibilities towards both the client (the person or company paying for the job) and the model. The agency stakes its reputation on every model it represents. That means it has a right to expect her to arrive on time for assignments, looking fresh and clean and alert. They expect her to be cooperative and efficient. Excuses, other than illness or a real emergency will not do. If a model lives up to her responsibilities her agency will protect her and if necessary, defend her against any unfair complaints the client might make.

71

For example, let us say you are scheduled to arrive at a job at nine o'clock in the morning. At 9:30 the agency gets a call saying you have not yet arrived or that you arrived looking as if you'd been up all night and that they can't possibly use you. If this happens and it is not true (on some few occasions a client may try to wriggle out of a set appointment) you'd better get over to your agency fast if you want to prove that it just isn't so.

If a client waits two or three weeks, however, before making a complaint, the chances are whatever went wrong was not your fault. The client may be looking for a reduction in the fee or perhaps has changed his mind about an ad. While this kind of thing doesn't happen too often you have every right to expect your agency to defend you. Most agencies will go to bat for their models as long as they know they have always been dependable.

THE BOOKING ROOM

A good agency provides a number of other services. The most important is performed by the booking room. You might call the booking room the heart of the agency. In it are half a dozen or more telephone operators whose job it is to keep track of all calls for each model. These operators make appointments, answer questions, take messages and keep track of each model's assignments. At any specific moment the agency should be able to track down a particular model through the booking room. Her work sheet will show exactly where she is working. The model, in turn, can check with the booking room to pick up important messages or to confirm a booking or get information about a promising go-see. It's the exchange of information between the model and the booking room that helps make the business work.

A client will call an agency for a specific model it knows is represented by that firm. Or else, they need a certain "type" they feel that agency can provide. In the latter case the agency doesn't play favorites. They may send as many as twenty girls for a single job. The nineteen who aren't selected must realize that the client has asked for a chance to choose from among a number of models.

72

If the agency thinks you're right for the job, they'll send you as well as others. But being "right" for any job is strictly the decision of the client. So be prepared to compete for jobs with models you see every day.

YOUR FELLOW MODELS

Which brings me to another important point. You will be seeing some of the same faces over and over again. Some of them may get a job you'd like to have. Don't bear any ill-will towards the other girls because a client wanted one of them over you.

Also try to keep an even-tempered attitude towards the agency personnel even though you may occasionally feel you are not being sent for jobs you might get. Keep in mind that these may be the people who gave you your first chance at professional modeling. They will take care of the many, many details you'll never have time for once your career gets into full swing. So they deserve your courtesy.

Once the agency sets up an interview for you, you are obligated to go. All the same rules apply that did when you were first interviewed by the agency. Be on time, be well-groomed and well-dressed. Since you are there looking for work you should bear that in mind. That doesn't mean acting as if you're desperate or as if you'll do *anything* to get the job. As a professional you have a reputation and an image to uphold.

I know it may be difficult to believe but models do turn down jobs. Although every model likes to work as much as she can every now and then she may get a job and not want it. Sometimes she has received a better offer for the particular time she is needed. Sometimes she has a previous commitment and can't take the job unless it can be rescheduled. At other times she may decide that a certain job might identify her too strongly with a specific product.

Whatever the reason, a successful model is always tactful about saying no. You might say a successful model knows how to say "no" with a "yes accent." Just because she doesn't want or can't take that particular job doesn't mean that she wouldn't like to work for the same client in the future. If the client is really set on a specific model he will often reschedule a photo session so that she can do it.

RESPONSIBILITY AND SENTIMENT

Sometimes a model becomes so successful that a former client can't afford to pay her increased rates. This can be particularly sticky if she has done a lot of work for him in the past. There may be a degree of sentiment involved. More likely, the client may feel that she "owes" him something. Remember, the agency sets your rates and your financial success depends not only on the *number* of jobs you do, but also on how much you get paid for each job. Since you are under contract to the agency, you can't go behind its back and promise to work for less money than it would charge another client. That's one of the reasons you've agreed to allow them to represent you—to handle your financial arrangements. So let them handle it.

REJECTION AND HOW TO HANDLE IT

The hardest thing for a would-be model to accept is being rejected by a top agency. Self-doubt starts creeping in and soon you may start wondering why you ever thought *you* could be a professional model. Banish these thoughts from your mind. Agencies can't represent everyone. So if you get turned down by one, set up an appointment with another. And another. No one can tell you when it's time to quit. Some girls set a time limit on their pursuit of a modeling career. If they don't get enough work to support themselves after six months or a year, they give up. Others quit when their money runs out. And others get part-time jobs to tide them over and keep at it for years.

If you are willing to work as a showroom or department store model you may have enough extra time in which to pursue a career in advertising or TV commercial modeling. This is a decision you will have to make for yourself. After being in the business for awhile, you may discover it isn't all you thought it would be. In that case, there is no reason to keep at it. Many girls are willing to work as part-time secretaries or typists because they really love modeling even though they only get a few assignments every couple of months.

74

Others just can't take the constant search for work coupled with the stress and strain of financial insecurity. Remember, if you did your best you have nothing to be ashamed of. You can go home with your head held high. After all, you *tried* and that takes a lot of courage.

For those just starting out, remember that your greatest asset is your determination to achieve your goal. Keep at it until you have exhausted every possibility. That way you won't leave any room for doubt or regret no matter what the outcome.

HOW MUCH DOES A MODEL EARN

How much does a model earn? The answer is a little bit like the answer to how high is up. The most truthful answer, however, is, "It varies." It does, greatly.

Let's start at the top. The models who earn the most money are those affiliated with the most important agencies—Wilhelmina, Ford and Stewart in New York followed by Zoli and Stone. Some models earn $100,000 a year and more—possibly a dozen or two. Another group of popular and successful models will earn between $25,000 to $75,000 per year. Some of these girls could probably earn more than they do if they worked 12 months a year but many will take a month or two off for traveling and relaxation which they certainly deserve.

The models connected with these agencies are paid at the rate of $60 or $75 per hour. A few get $100 per hour and some few others who have achieved a special reputation have their fees negotiated by the agency. They are the ones who get the highest rates but they do not necessarily make the most money overall.

A work assignment can be as short as one hour (the minimum) or it can extend to a full day with overtime. Some assignments continue longer than this.

If a model works a full eight hour day she is paid at a daily rate. Some models get five times their hourly rate; others have higher specified daily rates. Overall, a day's work brings a payment of from $300 to $500.

These rates are for commercial work. Editorial modeling is generally paid for at lower rates but these are subject to negotiation and depend on a number of different factors.

75

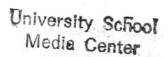

Modeling pay rates are lower in Los Angeles and Chicago than in New York and lower still in other cities. There is no doubt that New York is the modeling capital of the world.

There are a number of special situations which may add to the model's paycheck. While some girls may not wish to pose for lingerie ads, if they do they will receive a larger fee. Models with the largest agencies receive $250 an hour for bra, girdle or pantyhose modeling.

If an assignment is cancelled 48 hours or less before the scheduled time, the client must pay either a partial fee or the full fee. Overtime work, after a regular eight hour day, brings time and a half. Travel time is charged out at the regular rates or a portion of regular rates. A model is also paid for time spent having clothing fitted or for special hairdressing. If an outdoor session has to be cancelled because of inclement weather a W/P (weather permitting) rate goes into effect.

As I've said, while rates for the major agencies tend to follow this pattern, there are variations depending upon the location of the agency and the situations involved.

HEADSHEETS

Most agencies prepare headsheets which are sent to clients and potential clients. A headsheet is a booklet containing the photos (heads only) of the various models that the agency represents. It is a kind of catalog of their models currently available. In addition to the names of the models, other information is provided such as height, sizes worn and frequently their hourly and daily rates.

Additional information may also be included such as whether the model is a member of SAG or AFTRA (needed for television work), and the limits, if any, on the kind of bookings she will take.

THE COMPOSITE

A composite might be said to be a model's calling card. It can be prepared in a number of different ways. Some are printed as a four page brochure; others are oversized cards. A composite will have anywhere from two to eight photos of the model and contains her name, the agency which represents her, her measurements and clothing sizes (shoes, dresses, hats, etc.)

76

I use this photo in my large four page composite.

Wilhelmina, one of the most famous fashion models of all time, now heads a leading model agency under her own name.

viju
krem

One of my "calling cards."

Usually a model will want to have several hundred to a thousand copies printed. This is her responsibility although she will get advice from the agency people on photos to be used and the type of design.

The agency keeps a supply of each model's composite and sends them out, on request, to prospective clients who may have seen her photo first in the headsheet.

The model carries a supply of composites with her as she makes her rounds. If she is on a go-see, she will, of course, want to leave one, although the client may already have it. She will also want to leave a copy with various photographers, advertising agencies and other prospective clients. It is indeed her "calling card."

MODELING IN EUROPE

There are many modeling opportunities in Europe, particularly in cities such as London, Paris, Milan and Rome. Most major European cities have modeling agencies and I've included a listing of some of them at the end of the book. Many European assignments, however, originate in New York City and many American and some Canadian models are specifically asked for by clients in other parts of the world. And, of course, some of the leading models came originally from other lands such as Germany, France and the Scandinavian countries.

PHOTOGRAPHERS CAN HELP

Photographers often are helpful in forwarding a model's career. This is particularly true of the top photographers who select or are involved in the selection of models. Some of them have favorites with whom they have worked very successfully. Others, like agencies and clients, are on the lookout for new faces.

While there are literally thousands of lensmen everywhere who use models in their work, a handful of really outstanding photographers among them Milton Greene, Richard Avedon, Sheldon Secunda, Bert Stern, Francesco Scavullo, to name just a few, can play an important role in a girl's career. Sometimes, just the fact that one of these photographers has taken successful pictures of a new model has meant the blossoming of her career. Of course the top photographers have seen thousands of models and their standards are very high. It certainly does no harm, however, to mail your composite to various photographers. You may be just what one of them is looking for. Most studios discourage personal visits unless they have asked to see a specific girl but they do open their mail.

THE MODEL'S PORTFOLIO

You'll see many a girl trudging through the streets of New York with an oversized flat portfolio. If the girl is a model, and she usually is, it will contain a selection of her best photographs. If she is on a go-see she will want to show the client the work she has done and how she photographs in different kinds of costumes. In a way this portfolio is an expansion of the composite because she can carry many more pictures, usually blown up to twelve by sixteen inches or even larger. (Which accounts for the oversize portfolio.)

There may be pictures of her in a bathing suit, street clothes, sport clothes, some closeups of her face, some mood photos and whatever she regards as representing her best work. You are never quite sure of the kind of assignment the client is preparing so you must be ready to present a broad range of modeling situations.

Heather Hewitt, with Ford Models, found her career led to television and film work.

modeling in your hometown

You may think that all the modeling opportunities are in cities like New York, Los Angeles or Paris. While it is lovely to dream about being a glamorous model in some faraway city, in reality, you often don't have to pack your bags and leave home. Even if you eventually decide to make the big move, you can get a lot of valuable modeling experience right in your own hometown.

Personally, I would advise against any drastic move until you are certain about what you want to do. You should try to finish school before deciding on a full time career. If your parents are anything like mine, the thought of their daughter living all alone in a strange city doesn't exactly make them happy. And if you've tried to convince them that you don't *need* an education because you're positive that a successful modeling career is just around the corner, you've probably encountered some pretty strong parental resistance.

Unless you have saved some money on your own or your family can afford the expense of plane tickets, hotel bills and the necessities of life, while you make the rounds, it really is a lot to expect from them. If your parents are giving you a hard time it may be that they don't want to see you disappointed or unhappy.

THERE *ARE* OPPORTUNITIES

It's up to *you* to prove that you're serious about a modeling career. If you are being thwarted in your desires for a modeling career do something constructive. Seek out opportunities in your hometown and the surrounding area.

Do I hear a disbelieving groan? You don't think that there *are* modeling opportunities where you live? Well, you may be wrong! If your hometown has a department store there might be modeling jobs available there. The Y.W.C.A. or your church or social group can often be a source of modeling opportunities—even if you have to create them yourself. Don't overlook local charitable and civic groups. And the Chamber of Commerce. And your school.

There may even be a clothing manufacturer with a buyers' showroom somewhere in your vicinity. Then, there are local and state beauty contests that could lead to modeling. Some national magazines sponsor beauty contests. Let's talk about the many opportunities there are that can forward your entrance into a professional modeling career.

THE "GO-GETTER"

A successful model is a real "go-getter." She spends her time looking for all kinds of opportunities. Sometimes she is able to create them. A model in New York may have some advantages in being close to the heart of the fashion industry and the advertising field, but that doesn't mean that she started there. Successful models have come from all parts of the world. Many have told me that they took their first steps towards a modeling career long before they ever left home.

THE SAGA OF JENNY

I know a model named Jenny from such a small town that she is fond of saying, "By the time you're finished reading the Chamber of Commerce's welcome sign you're already through the town and past the city limits."

That didn't stop Jenny from making the most of every minute she spent there. For one thing she took a course at her local high school that really helped her career. Jenny decided to study public speaking.

"Viju," she confessed one afternoon while we were waiting for a set to be changed, "I was just about the shyest girl you ever saw. I had a terrible time getting up in front of people. Every time I had to read a class report I'd start stammering. I thought I'd just die of embarrassment."

That was hard to believe since Jenny is one of the most relaxed and poised girls I've ever known. Naturally I wanted to know how she got over her problems.

"I forced myself to do the thing I didn't think I was good at," she told me. "My biggest problem was learning to relax. When I found out that I could take a public speaking course in my junior year I decided to give it a try. Once I signed up for it there was no turning back. I had to give a speech at least once a week. Fortunately, the teacher was very understanding. She was also in charge of the school plays and she suggested that I try out for a part. At first I couldn't bring myself to do it. So I worked on the costumes and scenery for the first play. But we all had such a good time that I tried out for a part in the next production. I got it and it was really great."

Looking at Jenny I could easily see that getting involved has worked for her.

"I'm still taking voice lessons," she said. "As a matter of fact I think I've got a TV commercial lined up. I would never have gotten it if I hadn't started taking those public speaking lessons. If you get a chance tell the girls who read your book to tackle a problem like mine while they're still in school. Just trying to overcome a problem is better than running away from it. In my case it helped me gain the confidence I needed to be able to talk to people. I think I've talked myself into lots of jobs that I might not have gotten otherwise."

OTHER OPPORTUNITIES

There are lots of models like Jenny who had the good sense to take advantage of opportunities right under their noses. Another model told me about her high school days.

"I was terribly active in school. Not that I was a great student or anything, but after school I was into everything. I was a cheerleader and I was on nearly every sports team I could manage. One of the local department stores decided to do a big "back-to-school" fashion show and they wanted the cheerleaders to model some of the clothes. It was my first chance at modeling and I loved it.

"When it was over I asked the woman in charge if she thought we might do another show around Christmastime. She thought it was a terrific idea. This time I got to wear the evening gowns the store was selling for New Year's Eve. I guess that lady knew I was hooked because she asked me if I'd like to do another show in the spring. That store now does four shows every year using local high school students as models. I can't take credit for that but I do think that any girl who is really enthusiastic about modeling should talk to the fashion coordinator at her local department store. You never know what you can start until you try."

That's the whole point. You never know what you can start until you try.

SOME IDEAS FOR YOU

If you are a member of a club why not try to get a fashion show together. If you can't get a local department or fashion store to sponsor it, why not put on a show yourself? If your school has Home Economics courses you probably have a sewing class. Perhaps it would like to do a fashion show. The Y.W.C.A. often teaches classes in sewing and fashion design. Since they have facilities for seating large groups of people you may have a fashion show before you know it. Church and civic groups are always looking for good ideas for activities. They would probably love helping a group of girls model clothes. And if you make any extra money from it you'll know it's in a good cause.

While you're looking for opportunities don't pass up the less glamorous courses your school might offer. Business courses are always handy. A model usually can't hold a full-time job and still devote herself to her true career. Many models compromise by taking part-time jobs. Learning to type and take dictation may mean a way to earn enough extra money to make ends meet until your modeling assignments catch up with the cost of living.

I'm a great believer in after-school jobs. It's a great way to supplement your allowance (if you get one) and the only way to earn spending money if you don't. While baby-sitting is fine a would-be model may learn more from other jobs. Some cosmetic companies train high school and college students as campus representatives. Not only is it a great way to earn money but these companies teach how to apply makeup and they also sponsor beauty clinics.

Part-time jobs in department stores will give you a firsthand look at one aspect of the fashion industry and you often get an employee discount on clothes. Lots of department stores hire students during the summer months to act as salesclerks and fashion advisers for their back-to-school promotions. If you make a point of finding out what the store is doing to expand its youth market, you might be able to create modeling jobs for yourself.

I'm not suggesting that every outside interest you develop should be *calculated* to enhance your chance at a modeling career. I am suggesting, however, that you take stock of the amount of free time you have and how you spend it. I meet many girls who seem bored and complain that "there's nothing to do." That's ridiculous! Their real problem is that they don't make the effort to find out what they want to do and then take the trouble to do it.

In modeling, as in any other business, *you* are the one who has to make an effort. The world is full of people who manage to "get by." But successful models don't wait for things to happen, they make them happen. So open your eyes and look around.

MODELING SCHOOLS

I doubt that there is a would-be model who hasn't thought about going to a modeling school. These days you will find modeling or charm schools not only in major cities, but in many smaller cities and towns. Since it seems logical to want professional instruction many girls enroll in such courses every year.

As a professional I am often asked if I think these schools are worthwhile. I don't mean to dodge the question but I am not quite sure what "worthwhile" means to a specific individual. Just because you are a graduate of a modeling school is not a guarantee that you will become a professional model. However, many professional models *have* taken courses offered by these schools. Many feel that the instruction and guidance they received was indeed valuable.

Before you enroll in a modeling course you should make a thorough investigation of the school. While no one is able to give you an ironclad guarantee that you'll become a professional model, such schools often teach many things that are helpful to a novice. They place emphasis on makeup, hair care and other aspects of good grooming. They also give instruction on posture, carriage, showroom and fashion show procedures and generally offer information and guidance that might not otherwise be available to a would-be model.

Before you decide to spend a lot of money on a modeling course there are certain matters you should resolve. Write or call on as many schools as you can. If there is only one in your area, obviously you have no choice. If there is more than one, you owe it to yourself to investigate all the possibilities. Ask for their brochures and any other material pertaining to their courses.

Any reluctance on the part of a school to provide you with information may be an indication that something is wrong. When you receive the school's printed material, read it carefully. Make sure you understand what you're getting for your money. Beware of outrageous claims that promise fame and fortune to any graduate. Read the "fine print." And make sure you understand exactly how much the course will cost before you sign a contract or agreement.

I recommend that you visit the school before enrolling. It might be wise to take your mother or a friend with you. Then you'll have someone to discuss it with before you make a decision. If you are under legal age, let your parents know what you are doing since one of them will have to sign papers should you decide to enroll.

ASK QUESTIONS

Don't be shy about asking questions. Since many of these schools are quite expensive, you should get all the information you need to make a decision.

There are many opportunities today for black models. A black girl should not hesitate to ask if a school has instructors who specialize in teaching makeup and hairstyling for her racial group.

Make sure to ask if there are any "extras" needed to take the

86

course. If special makeup or clothing is required find out who provides it and if you are expected to pay an additional sum over and above the basic enrollment fee.

If the school promised to provide pictures, ask to see some they've taken of former students. It will give you an idea of how professional they are.

If the school has a placement service, find out if there is an additional fee. Since many schools claim that a number of their graduates have become professional models, try to find out if the school was active in bringing it about.

INSTANT SUCCESS?

I can't help feeling sorry for girls who expect instant success for their money. On the other hand I would never say that a modeling school *isn't* worthwhile. Many schools offer terrific courses that not only will help improve your personal appearance, but will give you real insight into the business. The success of any school depends largely on the competence of its instructors. If the instructors really understand what's going on in modeling today their assistance will be quite valuable. But if the instructors are locked into stereotyped ideas about how a model is "supposed" to look, you may be wasting your time and money.

Check the directory of modeling schools in major cities, along with model agencies, in the back of this book. Because one is listed does not mean I endorse it. They are there for your guidance and assistance. It is up to you to take the time to investigate those in which you are interested. If in doubt as to the legitimacy of a school call your local Better Business Bureau. The best way to discover the value of a course is to find girls who have taken it and ask them what they think.

Many girls who decide against, or can't afford, the more expensive modeling and charm schools take courses offered by local department stores and national chains like Sears and Wards. These stores offer basic self-improvement and charm courses at a modest cost. The store courses are very popular and can be a lot of fun as well as very helpful.

If you happen to be one of those lucky girls who lives in a big city (or in a nearby suburb) like New York, Chicago, San Francisco or Los Angeles, get out your local telephone directory and find out if any of your favorite fashion magazines have a local office. Lots of girls send pictures of themselves to the fashion and beauty editors of magazines and while this often doesn't bring a response, some magazines have used models selected from such photos. Many major publications do back-to-school issues, using students from high school and college campuses. If you are an avid reader of fashion and teenage magazines you have probably noticed that some of them sponsor beauty contests. Enter as many of these as you can. You never know what might happen.

BEAUTY CONTESTS

Speaking of beauty contests, call your local Chamber of Commerce and find out about local and statewide contests. The girls who compete for the Miss America title start by competing in local contests. While most girls are familiar with national and international beauty pageants it is surprising how few know that there are literally hundreds of local contests held every year. A lot of these contests are sponsored by resort areas or businesses that want to generate interest and goodwill. The contestant often has an opportunity to make personal appearances as a goodwill ambassador which, of course, is a terrific way to develop poise and a degree of stage presence.

Needless to say, you are the only one who can seek out these opportunities. Remember, a career in modeling doesn't just happen, you have to make it happen. So get out there and find out what's going on. Dreaming isn't nearly as nice as doing.

Instruction in makeup at the Barbizon School of Modeling

Getting ready to depart for a location assignment.

the big move

The girl who wants to become a successful model eventually must make a very important decision. Unless she already lives in or near a large metropolitan center where there are many opportunities for modeling, she has to go where the real action is.

While many large cities have jobs for models—Atlanta, Dallas, Washington, Detroit, Montreal—to name a few, there is no doubt that the big time and the big money is in New York City, the advertising and fashion capital of the world. The next largest selection of modeling opportunities in the U.S. will be found in Los Angeles, and Chicago. Los Angeles offers jobs in T.V. and has its own sizeable fashion industry, while Chicago is the home of a number of advertising agencies and the big catalog houses of Wards and Sears, although much of their fashion photography is done in New York.

If you are planning to move to New York or one of the other modeling centers such as Los Angeles, there is much planning to be done before you actually board the plane, train or bus for your trip. Most of this planning has to do with the costs of the trip and your living expenses while you are making the rounds of the modeling agencies and being interviewed.

91

First, find out how much the carfare is. If you are driving remember that a car is pretty much of a liability in New York. Parking is expensive and public transportation is much faster and cheaper. It's a lot easier to figure out the bus and subway systems than to drive around looking for a place to park.

In Los Angeles, however, a car is almost essential since there is limited public transportation and everything is spread out.

EXPENSES AND FINANCES

Your biggest and most important expenses will be for housing and food. But in your planning don't forget about carfares, makeup, and all the other little items that you are used to buying for yourself. It's a good idea to make a list and add it up.

Housing, however, is a prime consideration.

You may be lucky enough to have friends, or friends of your family, who live in the city and are willing to put you up for awhile. But before you descend on anyone, make sure the welcome mat is out. A friend of yours may have a small apartment. If you have never seen a New York studio apartment it may be quite a shock. While some are terrific, others are not much larger than walk-in closets. If your friend is living in one of those, a permanent houseguest can present problems. So plan accordingly.

If a friend has an apartment big enough for two (or more) and is willing to share it, you're in luck. Make sure, however, that you have a clear understanding of what it will cost. What will your share of the rent be? Since rent doesn't necessarily include utilities find out how much you will have to pay for gas and electricity. Leave room in your budget for a share of the telephone bill. You may find that you will need a phone of your own. A model has to be accessible and your roommate may be carrying on a marathon telephone romance.

If you don't know anyone who might put you up or can arrange temporary housing for you, you might have to stay in a hotel for a few days until you make other arrangements.

WOMEN'S RESIDENCES

However, better yet, for a girl just arriving in a strange city are the women's residences which are more moderately priced. They are usually run by religious or community organizations and in addition to being relatively low-cost, they are safe. Many aspiring models and actresses stay at these residences, at least until they have become more established and have a clearer idea of the way their careers are going.

I have included a listing of such residences in New York and Los Angeles at the end of this chapter for your guidance, but the scene changes and by the time you read this book there may be some new ones or some of those listed may have closed.

You can use the list, however, as a starting point. Write to them asking for rates and if there are any vacancies. Some residences are very popular and have a waiting list so you should plan your trip at least a month or two ahead.

If you want to get the most up-to-date information there are three organizations in New York City that will recommend places to stay.

They are: The Travelers Aid Society of New York City
204 East 39th Street
New York, New York 10016

The Federation of Protestant Welfare Agencies
281 Park Avenue South
New York, New York 10003

Catholic Charities
122 East 22nd Street
New York, New York 10010

But do remember to plan way ahead.

Travelers Aid maintains offices in 800 cities in the United States. If you ask your local chapter they will put you in touch with the proper organization in other cities to help you find such housing.

RESIDENCE SERVICES

Many residences have rooms with private baths and often the weekly price includes one or two meals. Some have light house-keeping facilities which means you can do your own laundry and whip up a midnight snack on the premises. You'd be surprised how much money you can save that way. However, the rates vary widely depending on facilities and you'll want to check with a few to compare rates and services.

Don't turn up your nose at the idea of a "woman's hotel." It may not be glamorous and some of the rules (like no men above the first floor) may not suit your new "big city" image, but they are convenient, less expensive than regular hotels and don't require a lease. They're full of girls just like you who have come to the city to make their mark in publishing, advertising, public relations, acting or modeling. Being with people your own age who are going through the same kinds of experiences can take the edge off a bad day. The girls who have been there for a while are more than willing to take a newcomer under their wings. It's nice to have a friend to go shopping with or someone to explore the city with.

YOUR OWN APARTMENT

After you have learned your way around and have established yourself, you may want to take an apartment. If you have a rapport with another girl or perhaps with two, it is much more economical to share an apartment. New York rents are high and usually you will have to sign a lease for a minimum of one year.

Los Angeles has lower rents and a number of apartments are available on a monthly basis. There are a larger number of furnished, or partially furnished apartments there than you will find in New York. The average New York apartment is unfurnished. Once you move in you will need everything from furniture to kitchen utensils.

There are companies which specialize in finding compatible roommates with whom you can share an apartment. While I cannot specifically recommend any one of them, you will find them listed in the Yellow Pages under Apartment Sharing Services.

Many girls already sharing an apartment learn that a roommate is moving out and the rent is too much to handle alone. They contact one of these services and interview prospective new roommates. In that case, you, as the new roommate, may move into a completely furnished apartment so that you have nothing at all to buy or you may only have to buy your own bed and chest of drawers.

APARTMENT ADVANTAGES

That's a lot less expensive than furnishing an apartment all by yourself. If you do have to buy a few things, try exploring the local thrift shops. It can be a lot of fun and a coat of paint can work miracles on an old chest. A couple of posters from a neighborhood store can also brighten any room.

There are certain advantages as well as disadvantages in taking an apartment.

Of course, it would be better to wait until you are well established and have a record of substantial earnings from modeling before you take an apartment on your own. Not only would you be committing yourself to a one-year lease but you will have to put out one or two months rent as security. If you have not been a previous customer both the telephone and electric companies require deposits. There are all kinds of small expenses incurred when you move into an apartment. Taken together they turn into one big expense. However, sharing these costs with one or two roommates makes life a bit easier.

One great advantage in an apartment is the fact that you will have a kitchen. Since meals taken outside, even in so-called inexpensive restaurants, tend to become a burdensome expense, the use of your own kitchen to prepare breakfasts and dinners can be a big saving. Naturally, you have to shop wisely, preferably once a week at a supermarket rather than picking up food items piecemeal from one of the numerous small groceries or "delis." Also, living in an apartment, surrounded by your own things, can be more comfortable and you won't be as tempted to spend money on outside entertainment.

NECESSITIES AND LUXURIES

It's difficult to anticipate every need when you move to New York. Sometimes it's hard to know what your top priorities should be. For example, the average girl with twenty-five extra dollars to spend might decide on dinner and a show. After all, New York has some of the finest theater in the world. But you might spend that money on a really good haircut. Ordinarily you would prefer to splurge but in this case I think the haircut is *more* important. You have to look good while you're making the rounds.

All of these things—necessities as well as a few small luxuries—take money. Since you are starting off on a fresh adventure without any certain knowledge of how quickly you will become a professional model and how successful you will be, you must be prepared to take care of basic expenses for at least two to three months. Time and money go very quickly.

Figure out how much money you have and how long it will last. You may have put aside some of your earnings from previous jobs. Perhaps your parents are willing to stake you for a few weeks or months. You must have enough in the bank or in traveler's checks before you leave home.

YOUR GREATEST ASSET – YOU

In any case, your greatest asset will be *you.* There may be some kind of work you can do while making the rounds.

There is a certain amount of part-time work available in most places and the key word here is part-time. The usual nine-to-five job doesn't give you the freedom to make appointments for the career you've set your heart upon. Plan on getting the best job available where the hours give you that freedom.

In New York and other large cities there are a number of employment agencies which handle part-time jobs. Typing or clerical work are good bets. You may be able to set aside a week or two for this kind of work and then take a week off to talk to model agency people. Or plan on working afternoons and leave your mornings free for interviews.

Analyze your skills to find out what kind of work you can do. Often something you have learned in the past comes in handy. One friend of mine was brought up in a French Canadian home and was fluent in French; another knew German very well. Both were able to get work tutoring students in those languages.

Department stores look for part-timers at different seasons of the year. Then, there always seems to be jobs for waitresses and these usually don't take the whole day. Jobs like these can help pay your basic expenses and supplement your original stake.

96

OTHER CONSIDERATIONS

There are other aspects of living away from home in another city that you should consider. You should think about the climate of the place you are headed for in order to take the proper kind of clothes. You know that Los Angeles never has any really cold weather and that New York and Chicago often experience bitter cold winters. Summer in those two places can also be terribly hot and humid. Your best bet before taking off for any place is to get a guide book to the area. You will learn a lot about the climate as well as other matters that will help you prepare for adjustments in your way of life.

If I plan to spend any length of time in any particular place, whether it be the United States, Canada, or Europe, I like to bone up on it. Besides providing me with interesting and often educational information, it makes the stay there much more pleasant and comfortable. So I suggest you do the same. In addition to the prime purpose of your trip, it will help you have fun.

I hope the suggestions I've made will help ease the inconveniences of the big move. Naturally, the anticipation of a new kind of life and the excitement of different and interesting surroundings will also give you the impetus to meet the challenge ahead.

WOMEN'S RESIDENCES IN NEW YORK AND LOS ANGELES

New York

Allerton House for Women—57th Street at Lexington Ave.
Baptist Residence for Working Women—225 East 53rd Street
Barbizon Hotel for Women—Lexington Avenue at 63rd Street
Jeanne D'Arc Home—253 West 24th Street
The Evangeline—123 West 13th Street
Parkside Evangeline—18 Gramercy Park South
Katherine House—118 West 13th Street
Milbank House—11 West 10th Street
Roberts House—151 East 36th Street
Sacred Heart Residence—432 West 20th Street
Sage House—49th West Ninth Street
St. Agnes Residence—237 West 74th Street
St. Dominic's Guild—203-209 East 71st Street
St. Joseph's Home—425 West 44th Street
St. Mary's Home—225 East 72nd Street
Simmons House for Women—350 West 88th Street
Swiss Town House—35 West 67th Street
Y.W.H.A.—Lexington Ave. bet. 91st & 92nd Streets
Hotel Martha Washington—29 East 29th Street
Webster Apartments—419 West 44th Street

Los Angeles

The Evangeline—1005 West 6th St.,
The Clark Residence—306 Loma Drive
International House—4952 Sunset Blvd.
Y.W.C.A.—The Hollywood Studio Club—1215 Lodi Place

98

diet and weight control

A successful professional model is constantly aware of one very basic aspect of her appearance. She knows she must maintain her ideal modeling weight. This is important no matter what her specialty may be. If you are serious about this career, you'll have to do the same.

YOUR IDEAL MODELING WEIGHT

Just what is ideal modeling weight? And what is yours?

Once you have reached the proper weight for your height and body frame, as indicated on page 26, you'll have to work from there. Your ideal modeling weight is that at which you look your best and photograph your best. You may know it yourself, or you may need the advice of friends or of professionals. There is no chart to follow. Even if you are the same height and have the same frame as another girl it doesn't mean that you'll have the same ideal modeling weight.

THE WAY YOU LOOK

Actual poundage is not as important as the way you look or the way you photograph. You use the indicator on your scale as a guide. Two girls, both five-feet-seven, are photographed. Even though they have the same general proportions, one finds she is 116 pounds; the other may be 112 or even 120.

99

Another photo used in my composite.

Much has been made of the fact that Margaux Hemingway, the modeling sensation of 1975 is heavier than she should be, or at least heavier than her ideal modeling weight might be thought to be. But she must photograph well because almost every magazine in the world wants her for a cover.

So, find *your* ideal modeling weight. And once you have, stick to it. Your scale with its pointer on *that* figure will be your guide for a long time to come.

HOW TO GET THERE

You may have to do a little work before you get there. Many girls, potentially good modeling material, are walking around with ten to twenty pounds too many.

If you are one of those, the first step will be to take off those extra pounds. Generally speaking, it is advisable to consult your doctor if you want to lose that much weight. He will make sure that going on a diet isn't going to harm you and he will probably suggest one.

Don't try to take off ten to twenty pounds or more in two or three weeks. Weight taken off too rapidly often causes the skin to sag and surely that won't help your modeling career. And while you are on your diet you will want to exercise to reduce those parts of your body on which the extra fat has accumulated.

I'm now going to assume that you've managed or are going to manage to get down to your ideal modeling weight. Since it is most important to stay there that is what this chapter is mostly about.

Those people who do manage to lose a fair amount of weight and are very proud of their accomplishment often seem to forget their original aim. Before long they've gained it all back. You can't do that if you want to be a model.

I've learned the hard way that you must keep a constant check on this department. The only way to keep this constant check is to step on your scale at least once every other day. If that pointer has moved upward, you must do something about it.

Like almost everyone else I have a fondness for rich foods, although I also enjoy simpler dishes. If I've been too tempted by some delicious offering like chicken in cream sauce or lobster pie or Viennese pastry and I discover that extra pound or two, I do something about it right away. When I do something about it I think I know what I'm doing. This is true of most of the models I know.

A SAD EXAMPLE

It seems, however, that no matter how much they may be told about it, some people never seem to understand which foods contribute to weight gain and which foods contribute to weight loss.

I'll show you what I mean.

It was one of those times when I had been to a number of holiday parties where a large array of tempting dishes were served at a buffet. On these occasions there is always the temptation to put more on your plate than you really want. Before I knew it, *wow*, two pounds. It seems I had neglected to get on the scale for most of the week.

I was doing something about it. I went on a diet immediately.

That very day I was having lunch in a restaurant with a friend, also a model, who must have been at some of the same parties.

At the next table were two very attractive women. As in many New York restaurants the tables were so close that we couldn't help overhearing their conversation. They were both dieting.

When the waiter took our orders, and theirs, it was only coincidence that the four of us ordered the same things—Chef's Salad and black coffee.

Our neighbors congratulated each other on being so virtuous. When their salads arrived, however, each of the women asked the waiter to bring an extra portion of Russian dressing. One woman calmly deposited two teaspoons of sugar into her coffee while the other used only one. Both ate the rolls and butter that had been placed on the table. And both decided that they were doing so well on their diets that a little lemon sherbert for dessert wouldn't hurt.

Let me tell you what happened at our table. When our salads arrived we asked the waiter to bring us lots of lemon wedges. No Russian dressing for us. It is made with mayonnaise, one of the most

102

fattening foods you can eat. Lemon juice can be a very tasty salad dressing and it certainly saves on calories.

No sugar in our coffee. A sugar substitute is close enough to the taste of sugar and saves even more calories. We ignored the rolls and butter. We ate our salads which consisted of pieces of lean chicken, ham and tongue and slivers of cheese with lots of salad greens.

Earlier for breakfast I had had half a grapefruit, a soft boiled egg, a thin slice of toast with just a touch of butter and some black coffee. Mid-morning I drank a glass of low-fat milk. That evening for dinner, a broiled hamburger patty made with lean beef, half a baked potato (no butter), a small portion of green peas seasoned with lemon juice, topped off by a whole apple.

This brought my total caloric intake for the day to about 1,000. Since I figure I must use up about 2500 calories in a day of dashing about town, the difference of 1500 calories would come from that extra poundage. A couple of days of watching my food intake and those two unwanted pounds would be gone.

I, and many of my friends, have been learning more about nutrition and the importance of calories, vitamins and other nutrients for health and beauty. You should, too.

While there are a number of different ways of maintaining or losing weight, I generally count calories.

FOOD AND CALORIES

Food is fuel for your body. All of us use up a certain amount of energy every day; this is measured in calories. If you take in more fuel (food) than your body requires for the day's energy, the excess will be kept in your body in the form of fat. If you take in less fuel, or food, than you require, the extra fuel is taken from the fat in your body.

Certain foods are very high in calories; others very low. For example, a good sized steak may contain from 1200 to 1600 calories. Add a baked potato smothered in butter or sour cream and you'll have another 300. On the other hand a tomato stuffed with cottage cheese on a bed of lettuce has about 200 calories. If you could eat a whole pound of lettuce you'd still absorb only 60 calories. (Much of lettuce is made up of water.)

In order to maintain your weight or lose weight you have to concentrate on the low calorie foods or eat much less of the high calorie foods. I suggest you get one of the many calorie charts or counters sold in book and stationery stores and consult it. (Unless, of course, you are one of those lucky ones who never seems to have a weight problem.) You may find that many of your notions of what is fattening and what isn't aren't quite right.

More and more women are becoming aware of the importance of good nutrition in their lives and its relation to their physical appearance. Obviously a model should be even more interested since her livelihood is at stake.

BASIC NUTRITION

If you don't do it now you should try to follow the basic rules about nutrition set down by the experts in the field. It is generally recognized that you should have servings from each of the four basic food groups each day. They are: a.) Fruits and vegetables, b.) Meat, fish, eggs, c.) Cereals (including whole grain breads,) d.) Dairy products.

Even when dieting you should be thinking of the four groups. You may notice that on the low calorie diet I was following after partying too much, I had some bread, meat, milk, fruit and vegetables. Something from each of the four groups. It isn't always easy.

By drawing on the four groups you will be getting the proteins, carbohydrates and fats as well as the vitamins and minerals that are so essential to sustain health and beauty. Robbing your body of all fats or carbohydrates because they are high in calories, if done over too long a time, may cause physical problems and affect your looks.

There was a time when many models would exist on cottage cheese and black coffee to keep their figures. This often resulted in drawn looks, skin problems and sagging skin. Not too good an idea. But, as I've said we are learning more about nutrition now.

CRASH DIETS

What about crash diets? Those on which you eat practically nothing. Fine, if you do it for two or three days. Much longer than that and you'll crash right out of your career. I've done it when I've had

104

to lose a pound or two quickly and so have many other girls. You do have to be careful, though. Such diets are very debilitating and you need your strength for those hectic assignments.

SOME MODELS' SLIMMING TECHNIQUES

Many models develop their own techniques for staying slim. I'd like to share some of them with you. Perhaps there are one or two you can use.

Several very successful models have gotten in the habit of eating only two meals a day, having a fairly substantial breakfast, no lunch at all except perhaps for a cup of bouillon or a glass of tomato juice, and then a regular dinner, skipping dessert. Ford model Shelley Hack has breakfast consisting of orange juice blended with an egg and banana, no lunch and meat or fish with vegetables for dinner.

Gunilla Knutson of Wilhelmina Models "takes it off" quickly with a Scandinavian diet which consists of breakfast of tea with honey, an apple at lunch and chicken broth for dinner. The next day she adds an orange to her breakfast, has some low calorie vegetables for lunch and fresh fruit and boiled rice for dinner. That's it. She says she can lose two pounds this way but can only stay on it for two days. She also takes a vitamin pill on those days.

THE HALFWAY MEASURE

My friend Louise, a lovely blonde with a warm, outgoing personality, is in demand for a lot of trade shows and conventions and they pay her top rates, too.

Louise has no trouble staying slim at home when she can control her meals. But working at a trade show is different. There's food everywhere. In the hotels, restaurants and hospitality suites (a room the client uses to entertain buyers), there are more than usually generous portions of foods. In addition she is constantly barraged by hors d'oeuvres at the many cocktail parties she is invited to. It really did her in.

But Louise figured out a way to keep things under control. I know she must have because her tall, angular body doesn't appear to have an extra ounce on it.

"It's easy to keep your weight under control," she said, "when you use the halfway measure. I just cut everything in half. Sandwiches are easy. I eat half and leave the rest. When I work in the hospitality suite I keep busy by filling everyone else's plate. That way I don't have time to eat.

"If I go out to dinner with a client and the buyers I just cut the whole meal in half. I eliminate an appetizer and have a cup of consomme. I order anything I like on the menu but I only eat half of what's on the plate. I order a salad and skip dessert. Since these people are there to discuss business nobody is interested in what I eat.

"My biggest problem used to be the before dinner drink. People get upset if they drink and you don't. So I order a glass of club soda with a twist of lime. And everybody's happy. Trade shows and conventions aren't a problem anymore."

Louise's "halfway measure" is terrific for a model working on location or in a studio where the lunch break usually means sending out to the local delicatessen for a sandwich. If you have to eat a sandwich, eat half of it.

THE EVERY OTHER DAY WAY

Another friend, Kris, uses a variation of Louise's "halfway measure." She eats almost anything (within reason) every other day. On the alternate days she restricts her food to 1,000 calories. Kris has figured out that she can have as many as 3,000 calories which might include that juicy steak and baked potato and other goodies on any one day as long as the following twenty-four hours are carefully watched. Nothing fattening.

MY FASTING METHOD

Whenever I have to lose a pound or two in a hurry I fast. I never do it for more than one day. And never when I'm working or have something strenuous to do. I wait until the weekend when I have little or nothing planned. I've learned from experience that I can't work without eating. All the rushing around makes me lightheaded. So when I fast I pace myself.

106

Fasting itself is easy. All I need is the time. And a supply of clear broth (bouillon cubes will do nicely) and lots of fresh lemons. I just don't eat. In the morning I have a cup of broth or bouillon. I spend the day reading or doing little things that I put off like writing letters or fixing a hem. I tried cleaning my apartment one day while I was fasting but I found that it was too strenuous. I got a terrible headache. So now I try to make fasting as relaxing as possible. During the day I drink all the water I want. If I'm in the mood I make fresh lemonade. I like it sour but I think you can use an artificial sweetener if you like.

SOME KEY POINTERS

Here are a few pointers for successfully controlling your weight. No doubt you've heard some of them before but a reminder never hurts.

Avoid fried foods. Instead have meat, fish and chicken—broiled.

Avoid regular soft drinks. Instead drink the low or no calorie versions.

Go very easy on desserts and candy. If you can get in the habit of not eating them, so much the better.

Use butter or margarine sparingly.

Take temptation out of your kitchen. Don't buy snack foods.

If you like to nibble on something during the day, prepare a plate of raw vegetables like carrot sticks, celery stalks, radishes, cucumbers, scallions.

Don't oversalt your food. Salt holds water and water retention will make you look and feel bloated.

Get in the habit of walking past the candy counter at the movies. At sports events ignore the peanut vendor. If you must chew on something try sugarless gum.

Drink a full glass of water before each meal. It helps fill you up and you'll probably eat less.

Avoid the coffee break habit. Keep some bouillon cubes with you and just ask for hot water in which to dissolve them. Drink the coffee, if you must, but drink it black. And, of course, no doughnuts or pastry.

Never eat just before going to bed.

Avoid sandwiches at lunch. Try soup and a salad instead. But if you do eat one, remove one slice of bread.

Do you like hamburgers. O.K. but without the bun.

Just remember to carry your calorie counter with you. Then, when you are tempted you can remind yourself by checking the calorie count of the foods you plan to order.

Just keep thinking how great you'll look if you maintain your ideal modeling weight.

Fresh fruits and vegetables are good for the complexion.

keeping trim

While watching the amount of food you eat and its caloric value is the best way to control your weight, exercise plays a very important role in keeping you trim. If you neglect to exercise while dieting you may find the pounds coming off in the wrong places.

Exercise doesn't have to be strenuous in order to be effective. But it should be regular. If you like to swim or ski or play tennis, that's fine, but if you can't do it on a regular basis, you should put a ten minutes a day exercise time into your schedule.

Actually, walking, if done at a reasonably fast pace, is one of the best exercises there is. I probably do more walking in my average day than most girls do in three or four days. It not only helps me stay slim but it keeps me in shape.

Of course I've always been interested in exercise, ever since I took my first ballet lesson. Then I had years of gymnastics.

Since I am one of those people who believes that one picture is worth a thousand words I have included some pictures of me in this chapter demonstrating some of the most effective exercises I know.

I've included an exercise that is great for tightening up your stomach muscles, one that really helps keep your waist trim, another that is terrific for hips and thighs, as well as one helpful in firming your bust.

These should be done every day, a few minutes for each of them.

I also suggest walking whenever you can, perhaps from one assignment to another if there is time. Bicycling is another non-strenuous exercise that is a lot of fun. A number of models I know use a bicycle in New York to get around.

Do remember, however, that a small amount of regular exercise every day will do you more good than an occasional weekend of hectic exercise.

Lie on your right side, support your head with one hand, and steady yourself with the other hand.

Slowly raise your left leg as high as you can, then lower it also slowly. Repeat five times. Then, turn on your left side and repeat the exercise, raising your right leg, five more times.

Crouch as low to the floor as you can.

Slowly raise yourself from the crouching position.

Keep rising until you are standing on your toes. Keep your arms at your side.

Still standing on your tip toes, stretch your arms over your head as high as you can. Remain there for a count of three. Then, return to your original crouching position and repeat the exercise five times.

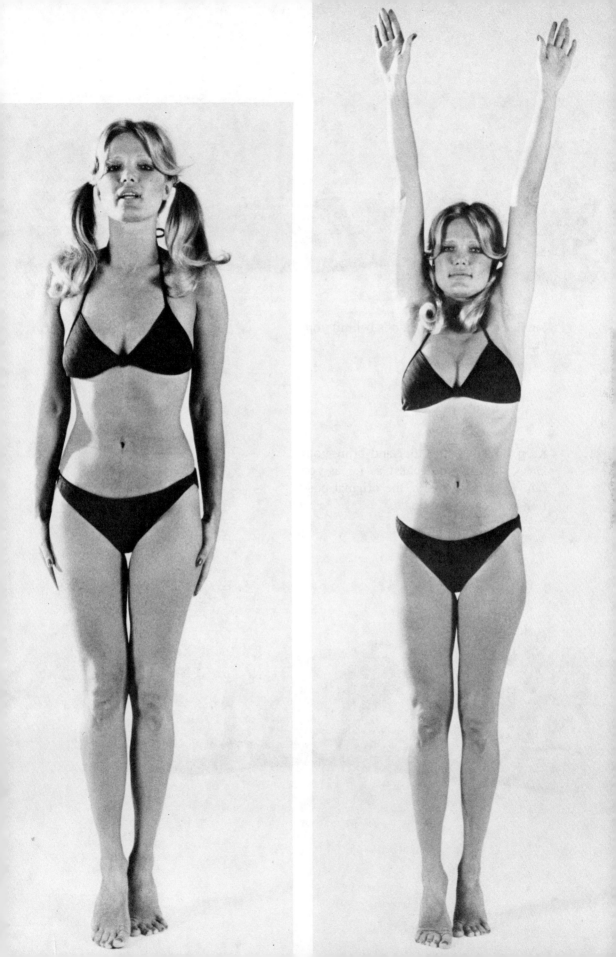

Lie flat on your back, hands behind your head.

Keep both legs together and bring your knees towards your chest as far as you can. Return slowly to the original position and repeat five times.

Support your hips with both hands and bring your legs over your head. Then move your legs in a rotating fashion as if you were riding a bicycle. Do this for at least one minute.

Again, lie flat on your back as in the previous exercise.

Raise your left leg, keeping it rigid.

Keep on raising it slowly until your leg is pointing as straight up as you can get it. Then, lower it slowly, holding it rigid. Repeat this five times. Then repeat the exercise raising your right leg.

Start once again from a prone position.

Keeping both legs together, raise them in a slow, even movement until they are pointing straight up. Repeat this exercise ten times.

Stand with your legs together, arms raised, finger tips touching as shown. Rise slowly on your toes.

Move your arms slowly to the side and rear as far as they will go. Repeat ten times.

Lie flat on your back, hands out-
stretched on both sides. Then raise your
chest as high as you can without moving
your hands. Hold your head as far back
as possible Count three and then return
to the original position. Repeat five
times.

Repairing my makeup in an improvised dressing room at New York's Cloisters (museum) before a fashion shooting.

Striking a pose for that fashion photo.

a day
in the life
of a model

I think what I like best about being a model is never really knowing what I'll be doing next. Since every assignment is a new adventure I never feel as if I'm in a rut.

I know that my lifestyle might drive another kind of person crazy. Some people need a regular job with regular hours. Not knowing what to expect can be pretty exasperating. But my life is irregular and frankly, I like it that way. Since I'm my own boss it's my responsibility to see that my part of the job gets done properly. I work for so many different people that sometimes life can get pretty hectic. That's why a model has to be a businesswoman and a diplomat too.

Before you leap into professional modeling you should take a good look at the kind of work I and others do. While it's true that some jobs are so well organized that a model can rely on a hairdresser and a makeup man to help her while she's working, generally speaking a model has to be a jack of all trades.

123

BEING FLEXIBLE

A good model has to be able to do the job under any and all circumstances and conditions. That means being flexible, handling anything that comes your way without getting uptight. Of course, experience is still the best teacher. But nobody can teach you the kind of outlook you'll need to become a successful model. You'll have to develop it for yourself. A sense of humor helps. So does being a willing and resourceful worker.

Being able to take things in stride is essential. The art of compromise is something else you'll have to learn. Being able to give in gracefully is a must (even when you know you are right). Being able to keep your cool while taking the same pose for what seems like the nine-hundredth time. Being able to take criticism without getting huffy. Being able to offer suggestions tactfully so that nobody else involved in the job looks bad. These are all things a model has to learn to do. When you think about it, aren't these the things we all *should* learn no matter what kind of work we do. I guess it's just a little tougher for us because there's so much money riding on each job. Time and money go hand in hand in this business. Our working conditions are often less than perfect. When things go wrong, people being what they are, tempers flare. The model who can't take it won't be asked back. The one who can, often saves the day with a laugh, a joke, or a helpful idea. Let me take you along on a few assignments and I think you'll get the picture.

THE NIGHT BEFORE

For me, every job starts the night before. I have learned that the time to prepare is before you start. On each night before an assignment I make sure that all my equipment is in my tote bag and ready to go. I carry a big, canvas tote with a handle and a shoulder strap. Lots of pockets and plenty of room. I prefer canvas because the bag itself doesn't weigh much. After you see the list of items I carry you'll understand why that's important.

Everybody asks what a model carries in those big bags. I guess it's natural curiosity since some of the most beautiful girls in New York can be seen carrying tote bags as well as portfolios. For a model it's as natural as carrying an ordinary handbag. Many a time I've received a kind offer from some unsuspecting gentleman who wants to help carry my bag. Usually they are shocked when they try to lift it. Mine weighs about twenty pounds and I don't carry as much as I used to. Just the essentials like:

    1 pair of black slacks
    1 black jersey evening dress
    2 tops (one sporty, one dressy)
    1 pair of evening slippers
    1 pair of plain black pumps
    1 bikini
    a jewelry case full of accessories
    a portable iron
    a curling iron
    a small hand hair dryer
    an extension cord
    a hairbrush and comb
    a complete makeup kit
    a folding mirror.

And of course, cotton balls and cotton swabs, plastic bottles containing nail polish remover and witch hazel, a manicure kit, a couple of extra pairs of panty hose (no heels or toes), a first aid kit with extra Band Aids, tissues, a head scarf, a short plastic cape, deodorant, dress shields, soap, a toothbrush and toothpaste, safety pins and a sewing kit, a sweater, a fringed silk shawl and sometimes, my lunch.

USING ACCESSORIES

No, I'm not planning a trip around the world—just a normal working day. I can take a pair of slacks and two tops and work with them to achieve at least a half dozen different looks by dressing them up or down. The same goes for the evening dress. My scarf becomes a belt. A necklace becomes a headband. With my hair up I can look chic and sophisticated. With it down I can look cute or sexy. My shawl becomes a prop. I can drape it over my shoulders or twirl it like a gypsy. A model learns to work with whatever is available. If you keep your eyes open, ideas begin to pop into your head. Almost anything can become a prop for a clever model. Often with dramatic results.

Of course, more often than not, the client has arranged for the clothing and accessories that I'm to wear. But, very often, a photographer will want to try some different photos so I'm prepared.

My tote bag is my tool kit. If I'm working tomorrow, I check it tonight. And if I'm out of something I replace it immediately. I've learned to take care of my equipment and it pays off.

Much of what I carry is the result of experience. A sewing kit has saved me more times than I can remember. An extension cord eliminates the aggravation that comes from trying to fix my hair when the nearest electrical outlet is ten feet away from the only mirror in the room while the cord on my curling iron is only three feet long.

Models work in the darndest places. Like shipyards or public parks. I've changed clothes in places you wouldn't believe. I've even redone my makeup while sitting on a horse. And that was a marked improvement over a couple of dressing rooms I've had. So I need what I carry, carry what I may need. I can't afford to run out of something when on location twenty miles from the nearest drugstore. Since your reputation is on the line every time you do a job—it pays to be prepared. Photographers don't like to be kept waiting. A client who pays you by the hour doesn't appreciate wasted time. A pro learns to work under any circumstance and make it tolerable.

PERSONAL RESEARCH

Once I've checked my bag I do some intensive research on myself, starting from the top and working down. Needless to say a model never works with dirty hair. I usually wash mine every other night. But if I am going on a job the next day I wash and set it that night.

Then I sit down in front of my makeup mirror and give my face a thorough going over. If I have any blemishes this is *not* the time to start performing do-it-yourself surgery. Luckily my skin rarely breaks out so the most I may have to do is gently remove an occasional blackhead.

126

I take the time to pluck any stray eyebrows the night before the job because I do it better when I take my time. It also allows at least twelve hours in which any red marks will fade.

I always do an extra thorough face cleaning the night before an assignment. Every model should take special care of her skin. I know I do. I always remove every speck of makeup every single night. That's standard procedure. But the night before an assignment I usually give myself a facial sauna.

HOW TO TAKE A FACIAL SAUNA

I do it the easy way by filling my bathroom sink with steaming hot water and then draping a towel over my head and bending over the sink for about three to five minutes of steam. After that a splash of cool water to close my pores. I wait about ten minutes before applying my regular moisturizer. Just before bed I apply a little more moisturizer. Since I know I will be using a lot of makeup the next day I like to baby my skin the night before.

Naturally, a check of legs and under my arms. I always shave very carefully—nicks and scrapes are a disaster. If I know I am going to be modeling bathing suits I usually try to have a professional waxing job. But if it's a last minute assignment, I shave. I've tried depilatories but they just don't do for me. Some girls swear by them but I like shaving better. It's just a matter of what works for you.

THAT COMFORTING BATH

By this time I'm ready for a long hot bath. Since I'm a bubble bath nut I toss a few capfuls of whatever I'm using into the tub and then fill it with hot water. Then I just lie back and relax for as long as possible. Sometimes I think about the job ahead but mostly I try to think of other things. I find it more relaxing to let my mind drift. Thinking about the job gets me uptight especially if I haven't worked with the photographer before or if I have to work with people I think may be difficult. If I do think about the job, I try to confine my thoughts to the clothes I'll be wearing or the product I'll be selling. Often I get some good ideas. But a model's ideas are often shrugged off. There are so many people involved in an assignment (each with his or her own concept) that often it's wiser to keep quiet and do what you're told.

One reason I like doing fashion work is because the photographer and the model often work alone. The one-to-one rapport can help turn out some beautiful pictures.

Television commercials are often complicated. Sometimes as many as thirty people crowd the studio and pandemonium may be the order of the day.

Since each job is different there is no point imagining all the things that might go wrong. And there's certainly no point thinking about all the things that have gone wrong. The ability to view each assignment as a brand new adventure makes my work more interesting. That way I bring a fresh approach to every job. So I lie back and relax. Whatever will be, will be.

HAIR CARE

Once out of the tub I blow my hair dry—almost dry that is—with a very powerful hand dryer. I use a warm setting, never hot. The force of the air will do the job. Using the hot setting causes my scalp to perspire and then the roots of my hair don't look clean. Being blonde, my hair has to look soft and shiny clean all the time. Even the tiniest bit of oil makes my hair photograph poorly. When my hair is just damp, I roll it up on huge rollers, as big as soup cans. Then I spend about twenty minutes under a hooded dryer (I prefer the kind with a hard top) and dry it thoroughly, still using a medium warm setting. My hair is very full but it is also very fine. That means it dries quickly. When it is dry, I unroll it and brush it out. I don't bother arranging it since I am going to sleep on it. I used to sleep with my rollers on but I wouldn't get a very good night's sleep and the roller marks often showed. So, in the morning I rely on a mist curling iron (the one in my tote bag) to tighten up the set.

THE MANICURE

While under the dryer I give myself a manicure. Since I'm in the habit of using a nail cream every night and pushing my cuticles back with a towel every time I wash my hands, manicures are easy. I just

128

smooth away any rough edges and apply polish if I think it necessary. I don't wear colored polish all the time. It chips easily and I don't have time to redo my nails on the job. I prefer a clear, colorless polish for everyday wear. Unless a color is requested my nails stay natural looking. If I do wear polish I tuck the bottle in my tote bag, just in case.

FOOT COMFORT

Once my hair is dry and I'm free to move around again, I give myself a pedicure. With all the walking I do, I have to take good care of my feet. I keep my toenails cut straight across and file away rough edges with an emery board. Since I make sure all my shoes fit, I don't have any corns or calluses. However, if I see one starting to develop I rub it gently with a pumice stone. Rough skin is murder on panty hose. Even though I carry two extra pair, its easier to avoid problems, than deal with them in the middle of a job.

By now I'm ready to relax before going to sleep. I usually read for about half an hour. The night before an assignment I make sure to get at least eight hours sleep. All the time and effort in the world can't make a tired face beautiful. Besides, we have a tough day tomorrow.

AT THE CRACK OF DAWN

How do you like getting up at the crack of dawn? If you want to be a model, you'd better get used to it. I'm one of those lucky people who wakes up the minute her feet touch the ground. I usually do about ten minutes of light exercise after I get up. Just some stretching and bending. Like the exercises I've shown you.

If you're one of those who takes an hour to wake, I suggest you get up an hour earlier. (Go to bed an hour earlier to compensate.) A tired model is hardly an asset to any job.

After a quick shower, I have a glass of juice and a cup of tea while I do my face. Ordinarily I don't use a lot of makeup, just a light foundation, a little eye makeup and some blusher. I think of my everyday makeup as a bare coat. The rest goes on at the studio after I find out what's necessary. Some models wouldn't be seen in public without their false eyelashes. I carry a couple of sets in my tote bag but don't wear them every day.

Most of my time is spent on my hair. I wear it down around my shoulders for a soft, natural look. Since I set it the night before, all I have to do is brush it out and arrange it. Like most models these days I rely on a good haircut. That way my hair falls into place without too much fussing. Most models wear their hair chin length or longer. The longer it is the more you can do with it. Of course wigs, switches and falls are so real looking that a model can wear her hair as short as she likes. But I think that if you are just starting out you should stay with a medium length cut. It's much more versatile. If you cut your hair very short it may take forever to grow back. When my hair won't behave, I use a curling iron to get the look I like. It's faster than electric curlers and I find it much easier to handle.

Getting dressed doesn't take long. These days, as I've said before, models wear whatever they like. Jeans, T-shirts, pants suits, whatever! The old image of a model wearing a "good little suit" complete with hat and gloves and carrying her hat box is somewhat hysterical. Believe it or not some girls still show up at agencies for an interview dressed that way. They must get their ideas from old movies on the Late Show.

Don't get the idea that I'm saying that good grooming is a thing of the past. Far from it! I think today's models look better than ever. It's just that they look a lot more real. If you look through magazines you'll see that fashion layouts are more realistic. The models are usually doing the kinds of things you'd be doing if you bought the clothes they're wearing.

When I get dressed to go to work I'll bet I'm not wearing anything very different from some of the things you've got in your closet.

As I've said, when you get around to going on your first interviews don't try to look *like a model*. If you do, chances are you'll be overdressed and uncomfortable. Just make sure whatever you wear is neat and clean. And make sure your clothes fit.

A PHOTOGRAPHER CAN BE A FRIEND

Not long ago I was working with a photographer who told me an incredible story about a girl who called his studio and asked if he was testing (if he was experimenting with some new ideas or equipment).

130

A lot of photographers will take pictures of a new model because they want to try out a new camera or some new ideas. It's really the best way to get professional pictures. You give him your time and he gives you some free pictures. Everybody's happy.

This photographer *was* testing and he asked the girl to his studio. She arrived looking like she'd been caught in the middle of a war. She actually expected the photographer to take pictures and she wanted prints for her portfolio. When he tactfully suggested that pictures of her looking the way she did wouldn't be very flattering, she said, "But I don't *always* look this way." It just didn't make sense. Whatever she usually looked like didn't matter. He only remembers what he saw and it was quite enough, thank you.

A photographer can be a great friend. If he likes you he is in a perfect position to recommend you for a job. Lots of clients trust a photographer's judgment to the point where the photographer can hire a model of his choosing. Every model I know has gotten some work because a photographer has recommended her. While it may not be the ideal situation, a lot of your modeling success may be based on who you know. It pays to make friends while you work. I don't mean that you need friends like the guy I mentioned earlier who offered me a job if I would be *nice* to him. I mean real friends who respect your work and can give your career a helpful nudge every now and then because they think you're good at what you do.

Some models get reputations for being aloof. Maybe they act that way because they've had some bad experiences with pushy people who like to associate with beautiful women. But that doesn't give them the right to take it out on their co-workers. An assignment is not a social occasion but that doesn't mean that you toss your manners out the window when you go to work. The model who pushes past the receptionist without so much as a good morning is rude. If she gushes all over the client and the photographer and treats the technicians like dirt she's a phony and everybody knows it. If she cultivates the "important" people involved in an assignment and makes everyone else feel insignificant she's well on her way to developing the kind of reputation that won't do her any good. So treat the people you work with the way you treat your friends. If you're lucky they'll treat you the same way. Even if they never help you professionally you've gained something valuable.

On an assignment on a hot summer day and I dress as comfortably as possible. I check the building directory for the location of the photographer's studio.

Entering the studio with what I hope is a pleasant greeting.

I check with my answering service and agency several times during the day, no matter where I am.

Not all studios are as well equipped as one would like, so I spread my own equipment on the dressing table.

THE BEST ASSIGNMENTS

A lot of people ask me what kind of assignments I like best. As a model, I judge assignments two ways. To be honest, those I like best are the jobs where I can earn the most money. That naturally puts TV commercials at the top of the list. Some models have lived comfortably for a year on the residuals from a commercial that took three days to make. But TV commercials are the most difficult jobs to get so like most models I take a lot of different assignments. Because of my background and interest in fashion design, I would have to say that I like doing fashion work best.

On a day to day basis, however, I have a different way of judging assignments. Those I like best are done in the most organized and professional way possible.

I also prefer to work with as few people as possible. Not because I don't like people. I may like them too much. But the more people on a set, the more confused a model can become. I'd much rather work with a photographer who knows what he wants than a whole group of people with lots of ideas. A model has to take directions from one central figure or the job can disintegrate into a disorganized mess. I sometimes think of my assignments as a play and each person involved as having a different role. The best assignments are those in which everybody knows his part and plays it to the best of his ability.

Most models find it terribly distracting (and sometimes downright embarrassing) to be caught in the middle of an argument over the creative concept of an ad. Everybody talks and nobody listens. And the model stands withering under the lights trying not to muss the clothes. That can be a real drag. It's a great opportunity *not* to get involved, too.

A TYPICAL ASSIGNMENT

A typical assignment goes something like this. I arrive at the studio when expected or even a few minutes early. Let's say it's for photographs for an advertising insert a department store will send with its customers' bills. Envelope stuffers provide a lot of modeling jobs these days.

134

The clothes are ready and so are the accessories. I chat with the photographer about which outfit he wants to do first and check with the stylist to see which accessories go with each outfit. Then I head for the dressing room. Since I'll be modeling a pants suit first there's no need for a lot of dramatic makeup. I touch up my face, arrange my hair and then I get dressed. I've learned never to take a chance on ruining clothes by wearing them while putting on makeup.

The shoes I'll be wearing in the picture are already on the set because I'll be standing on a sheet of seamless paper and no dirty footprints must show. I go back to the set, and before stepping carefully onto the edge of the paper, remove my own shoes. The stylist checks the outfit to see that it looks right and that no labels show unless they're supposed to. She makes sure there are no specks of lint or strands of hair on the fabric.

If a hairdresser is present he or she may touch up my hair but with soaring costs these days, hairstylists are only used on jobs with really big budgets. If the clothes need pinning or alterations of any kind on an assignment like this the stylist does it. One of the reasons most outfits are photographed straight on is because the back is often a mass of pins and clips. But once the clothes *look* right, we start shooting.

The photographer tells me what kind of "look" he wants and I do my best to give it to him. As soon as we finish one outfit we start on the next. The hardest thing to remember with all the hurrying is to not step on and off the seamless paper wearing the same shoes. If the paper gets smudged it takes time to replace.

I may change clothes and hairstyles half a dozen times before we finish the assignment and the pace is steady. If everybody is doing his job we work quickly. But if we have to stop because a necklace has been lost or a hem needs fixing it breaks the rhythm of the session.

READY TO LEAVE

When the last outfit has been photographed I head back to the dressing room and get ready to leave. Before leaving, however, the photographer signs my voucher book and I sign a release. The signed voucher will go to my agency which will record the number of hours I worked and is the basis for billing the client. Sometimes the voucher is signed by the client or his representative.

It takes about fifteen minutes to cleanse my face, reapply my makeup and get dressed. Then I'm on my way to the next assignment. Most of a successful model's days are spent in a similar manner.

My first job may start at nine in the morning and go until two in the afternoon, but that doesn't mean I'm through at two. I may have another job starting at 2:30. It doesn't leave much time. Which is why I sometimes carry my lunch in my tote. You'd be surprised at how many lunches I've eaten in the back of a taxi while hurrying to my next assignment.

LOCATION ASSIGNMENTS

On other days an assignment might take me on location, perhaps to do outdoor photography, in or around New York City. Fashion shots are often done using an attractive backdrop such as the steps and facade of the Metropolitan Museum of Art or the Public Library. At times we can be photographed in Central Park with the New York skyline in the background.

WONDERFUL TIMES – SLOW TIMES

Then there are those wonderful times when a client will fly me and a few other models to a Caribbean island or to Mexico for special photography in which those settings become the stage for an ad or brochure.

Naturally there are those days when there are no specific assignments. They counterbalance the sessions that run into the late evening hours, sometimes as late as midnight for which, of course, the client pays an additional fee.

On a very important job where a client is looking for perfection the work may continue for several days. And then there are the briefer sessions of one or two hours in which a client with a limited budget wants to squeeze everything possible into that time.

136

I think you see what I mean about no day being like any other, which is why I find the work so exciting. However, no matter where I am, Mexico or New York City, I have to keep in constant touch with the agency. They've been handling my bookings for the days and weeks ahead and hopefully there are plenty of go-sees lined up.

Remember I said a model has to be a businesswoman too. That means keeping your appointment book up-to-date. It means checking with your agency and your answering service, if you have one. And of course, returning calls. A photographer may have a job or a lead. A manufacturer may want me to do a show. Or a casting director may have liked my composite and want me to come in for an interview. You never know.

One thing I do know is that my days, and those of most successful models, are long ones. Sometimes I'm tempted to let things slide. But I can't and neither will you if you want to be a success. You have to follow every lead, no matter how tired you are. If you don't there is always another model who will.

The job you do today may have to tide you over to the next. Not being able to pay the rent isn't very glamorous. And having a stack of unpaid bills is a bad scene. I've always felt that having financial worries can be a jinx for a model. If a girl needs a job desperately and shows it, the chances are she won't get it. If she's worried about money it will affect her approach. That's the reason it is important to learn to budget money. That way one never feels desperate. Jobs seem to go to the happy, relaxed girls who haven't a worry in the world. Or so it seems.

Don't get carried away. Pay your bills first and pay the rent. Don't leave your paycheck in a manufacturer's showroom. The manufacturer is often kind enough to offer to sell you clothes at wholesale prices. It's probably a model's biggest temptation. You *are* getting a terrific bargain—if you know how to buy what you will wear. If you go overboard and start buying out the showroom you'll wind up with a closet full of last year's clothes and more than likely a drawer full of last month's bills. I ought to know, I've done it myself. I learned through experience to resist the temptation in accepting these offers and to say no thanks, unless it is something I would have wanted to buy anyway.

The next day isn't a work day and I have
accepted an invitation for dinner at the
renowned "21" and take the opportunity to admire the outside decorations
before entering the club.

My normal working day ends about five-thirty in the afternoon. By then I've answered all my calls and made a list of the people I didn't reach so I can call them first thing in the morning. I am ready to relax—probably for the first time all day.

Believe it or not, most models don't date much during the week. Just think—all those attractive girls sitting home with a good book. If I do go out in the evening I have to make it an early date. There is no way I can dance until dawn and then get up and go to work. So, it's mostly a light supper and a quiet evening for me. I save my socializing for the weekends or for evenings when nothing is set for the next morning. Naturally, with an early assignment I check my tote bag and go through the procedure I described at the beginning of this chapter to start getting ready for whatever tomorrow may bring.

All in all it's an interesting and varied life, but I've learned that it's important to keep on your toes. You will, too.

Gary Bernstein

Cynthia Swearingen, a Wilhelmina model, has been featured in many cosmetic and fashion ads.

male modeling

Male modeling in America has been very lucrative recently, not only for the all-American handsome boy, but also for the rugged character types. The field is open for almost any type of look, as long as your look fits the product. Catalog work, advertising ads, fashion shows and T.V. commercials are all open to male models. Because, basically, there are no schools for men who want to be models, guts and acquiring experience are really the necessary ingredients. The men in modeling do seem to have it made in one sense; they don't have to know all about makeup and the rest of that rigamarole that girl models have to go through. For male models, being tall and assertive, with a strong personality and a knowledge of the "type" that you are, and making the most out of what you've got, are really the main points to remember to become successful. More and more young men are becoming interested in the modeling profession, even though they hold other jobs. You'd be surprised how many cab drivers, waiters, plumbers, firemen, policemen, all ranging from the ages of 15—

50, call me for advice on modeling. My only advice to them is that, if they truly believe they qualify, and if they are confident enough in themselves, they should get some great pictures together, have them blown up, and take them to some of the agencies I mention at the end of this book; then, if the agencies like the photographs enough, they will advise the prospective model to get composites made up. It's the same thing as in female modeling—pictures, pictures, pictures tell the tale. And if you can show yourself in as great a variety of different looks as possible—from the all-American, rugged, sophisticated, high fashion, at apparently different ages, with a beard, a moustache (or whatever you can dream up)—then, the better off you are. This will show your talent and versatility to the client when he sees your composite. Some male models, who are also actors, will have a composite and a ''glossy'' with a resume in the back, so that the most suitable picture is left to the choice of the photographer or client. This should increase your chances of getting the job.

It is a good idea, and advantageous, to do some testing for your composite and portfolio with female models, because a lot of jobs use male models with girls in fashion photographs or ads. Also, the male model's job may be to enhance the girl, if she is doing a fashion or commercial shot; and, of course, girls can recommend you for certain jobs if they have tested with you, and you find it easy to synchronize your movements and work well together. Arrange interviews with some of the top men's fashion design houses. It is very prestigious and steady work if you are modeling for Jacques Belloni, Valentino, Bill Blass, Scott Barrie, Noi or Kenneth Lane. And they do quite often stage fashion shows, usually about twice a year, which can be a lot of fun. Film productions are using lots of models these days, often as extras and for small parts, but for work in that area it is preferable to be with a talent agency. Many models these days are with several agencies, and are working with them on a non-contract, free-lance basis. For example, for modeling you could be with a straight model agency, then get tied up with a couple of talent and commercial agencies. This will give you a variety of work which will make your job more interesting.

As far as staying slim and taking care of yourself with enough rest, so that you are bright-eyed and bushy-tailed—the same rules apply as for female modeling. Keeping your weight down by working out at the gym is a good idea, and what a lot of male models do. There's nothing like a good strong, but trim body on a male model. Being tall is also very important,

142

even though commercials sometimes use shorter men, if you are a character type. A good complexion is a must, so it is important to use cleansing and toning lotions regularly. The kind of clothes suitable to wear for an interview is another important factor. You should wear the colors that suit you best—solid, simple and elegant; even though until now male models have gotten away with wearing good jeans, just like the girls. You should remember, though, that if you are different, sometimes it can be to your advantage when you are job-hunting. To know what to wear for each particular job is important. You should get all the details from your agent, so that you can discuss how you would look your best. You should have a variety of clothes in your wardrobe, because often you have to use your own for jobs. Having a good personality and being friendly is as important for a male model as it is for a female model. Nobody wants a grouch or problem-seeker on the set, so learn to be helpful and flexible. A smile goes a long way, and comes across on a camera.

Parading down the runway in a typical fashion showing.

model agencies and schools

The following list of agencies and schools is as complete as possible. There are, however, some others, not listed, which may have been established after the list was compiled. Except for the well-established agencies and schools, many are short-lived and may no longer be around by the time you read this book.

You can confirm whether or not you ought to get in touch with any of those listed by checking the telephone directory of the particular city in which you are interested.

The code letters following the name will tell you whether it is a school (MS), agency (MA) or both (MAS).

ALABAMA

Birmingham

Birmingham Models & Talent (MAS)
A Division of Sylvia Pittman's
  Mannequins, Inc.
2001 Eleventh Avenue South
Birmingham, Alabama 35205

Huntsville

Nell Wond Modeling School & Agency (MAS)
South Memorial Parkway, Haysland Shopping Center
Huntsville, Alabama 35802

ALASKA

Anchorage

John Robert Powers Finishing School (MS)
750 West 2nd Street
Anchorage, Alaska 99501

ARIZONA

Phoenix

Abetter Agency (MA)
3033 North Central 206
Phoenix, Arizona 85012

Barbizon of Phoenix (MS)
1647 A West Bethany Home Road
Phoenix, Arizona 85016

Plaza Three Modeling & Finishing School
  & Talent & Modeling Agency (MAS)
4343 North 16th Street
Phoenix, Arizona 85016

CALIFORNIA

Anaheim

Barbizon School of Modeling (MS)
2093 East Ball Road
Anaheim, California 92806

Beverly Hills

Flaire Agency (MAS)
155 South Robertson
Beverly Hills, California 90021

Carlsbad

John Robert Powers School (MS)
Plaza Camino Real Shopping Center
2525 El Camino Real
Carlsbad, California 92008

Cerritos

John Robert Powers Finishing
  & Fashion Modeling School (MS)
401 Los Cerritos
Cerritos, California

Covina

Studio Seven Agency (MA)
261 East Rowland Avenue
Covina, California 91723

Fullerton

Tram Star Productions (MA)
P.O. Box 2669
Fullerton, California 92633

Hollywood

Caroline Leonetti (MAS)
6526 Sunset Boulevard
Hollywood, California 90028

Los Alamitos

Barbizon School of Modeling (MS)
10900 Los Alamitos Building, Suite 208
Los Alamitos, California 90720

Los Angeles

Barbizon of Los Angeles (MS)
3450 Wilshire Boulevard
Los Angeles, California 90010

CHN International Agency (MA)
7428 Santa Monica Boulevard
Los Angeles, California 90046

Exquisite Modeling School & Agency (MAS)
4315½ Leinert Building
Los Angeles, California 90008

Fran O'Bryan Agency (MAS)
600 South San Vicente Boulevard
Los Angeles, California 90048

146

Nese Photography Agency (MA)
5537 North Figueroa Street
Los Angeles, California 90042

Nina Blanchard Agency (MA)
1717 North Highland Avenue
Los Angeles, California 90028

Show Talent International Agency (MA)
Artist's Manager
831 North Fairfax Avenue
Los Angeles, California 90046

Newport

Dorothy Shreve Modeling School & Agency (MAS)
3404 Via Lido Newport
Newport, California 92663

Palm Desert

Cindy Romano Finishing School &
   Modeling Agency (MAS)
P.O. Box 1951
Palm Desert, California 92260

Pasadena

William Adrian Original Teen Models Agency (MA)
520 South Lake Avenue
Pasadena, California 91101

Redondo Beach

John Robert Powers (MS)
1509 Hawthirne Boulevard
Redondo Beach, California 90278

Riverside

John Robert Powers (MS)
3603 Plaza Mall
Riverside, California 92606

Santa Ana

Ed Harrell Studio of Charm & Modeling (MAS)
1519 North Main Street
Santa Ana, California 92701

Santa Barbara

La Belle Agency (MA)
El Paseo Studio III
Santa Barbara, California 93102

San Diego

Barbizon of San Diego (MS)
452 Fashion Vallen
San Diego, California 92110

Fashion Institute of San Diego (MAS)
Fifth Avenue Agency
1727 Fifth Avenue
San Diego, California 92101

John Robert Powers School (MS)
525 B Street
Suite 510
San Diego, California 92101

Tina Real Agency (MA)
Artists' Manager
3108 Fifth Avenue, Suite B
San Diego, California 92103

San Francisco

Barbizon of San Francisco (MAS)
240 Stockton on Union Square
San Francisco, California 94108

Brebner Agency (MA)
Models Division
1615 Polk Street
San Francisco, California

Fugate Agency (MAS)
Division of House of Charm School
157 Maiden Lane
San Francisco, California 94108

Girl Power Agency (MA)
166 Geary Street
San Francisco, California 94108

James Grimme (MAS)
41 Grant Avenue
San Francisco, California 94108

La Vonne Valentine, Modeling & Acting
   School (MS)
2113 Van Ness Avenue
San Francisco, California 94109

Torrance

Alese Marshall (MA)
4309 Messa Street
Torrance, California 90505

San Jose

Barbizon of San Jose (MS)
3033 Moorpark Avenue
San Jose, California 95128

147

Walnut Creek

Madeline School of Fashion Modeling (MAS)
1513 North Main Street
Walnut Creek, California 94596

West Los Angeles

Andre Duval Model Agency (MA)
1100 Glendon Avenue
West Los Angeles, California 90024

John Robert Powers Finishing & Fashion
    Modeling School (MS)
1100 Glendon Avenue
West Los Angeles, California 90024

COLORADO

Denver

Hopkins Talent & Modeling Agency (MA)
640 Sherman Street, North Suite
Denver, Colorado 80203

J.F. Images (MAS)
1776 South Jackson
Denver, Colorado 80210

Englewood

Barbizon School of Modeling & Agency (MAS)
Cinderella City, E. 1310
Englewood, Colorado 80110

Fort Collins

Kerver People (MA)
315 West Oak, Suite 601
Fort Collins, Colorado 80521

CONNECTICUT

New Haven

Barbizon of New Haven (MS)
419 Whaley Avenue
New Haven, Connecticut 96511

Stamford

Barbizon of Stamford (MS)
760 Summer Street
Stamford, Connecticut 06901

Connecticut Modeling Agency (MA)
1326 Shippan Avenue
Stamford, Connecticut

Westport

Joanna Lawrence Agency (MA)
82 Patrick Road
Westport, Connecticut 06880

FLORIDA

Coral Gables

Allegro Modeling School (MS)
276 Miracle Mile
Coral Gables, Florida 33134

Barbizon of Coral Gables (MAS)
223 Aragon Avenue
Coral Gables, Florida 33134

Charm Modeling Agency (MA)
333 Alcazar Avenue
Coral Gables, Florida 33134

Denson Modeling Agency (MA)
276 Miracle Mile
Coral Gables, Florida 33134

John Robert Powers (MS)
220 Miracle Mile
Coral Gables, Florida 33134

Fort Lauderdale

Atlantic Agency, Inc. (MA)
3038 North Federal Highway
Times Square, Building L
Fort Lauderdale, Florida 33306

Barbizon School of Modeling (MS)
Fort Lauderdale Division
1750 East Commercial Boulevard
Fort Lauderdale, Florida 33308

Florida Talent Agency (MA)
2631 East Oakland Park
Fort Lauderdale, Florida 33306

Gayle Carson Career School (MS)
3925 North Andrews Avenue
Fort Lauderdale, Florida

148

Hollywood

Charm Modeling Agency (MA)
4238 Hollywood Boulevard
Hollywood, Florida

Jacksonville

Barbizon of Jacksonville (MS)
Barnett Regency Tower
Suite 210 at Regency Square
Jacksonville, Florida 32211

Key Biscayne

MarBea Talent Agency (MAS)
Key Biscayne School of Modeling
104 Crandon Boulevard
Key Biscayne, Florida 33149

Merritt Island

Patricia Stevens Modeling School
  & Agency (MAS)
262 East Merritt Island Causeway #14
Merritt Island, Florida 32952

Miami

Appleby Photographics (MA)
7370 Bird Road
Miami, Florida 33155

Fashioncrest International (MAS)
777 N.W. 72nd Avenue
Miami, Florida 33126

The Glen Jones School of Fashion Arts (MAS)
Glen Jones Models
777 N.W. 72nd Avenue
Miami, Florida 33126

Miami-Dade Community College (MS)
Ms. Lorna Davis
South Campus
11011 S.W. 104th Street
Miami, Florida 33156

Miami Beach

American Models Association of
  Miami Beach (MA)
19400 Collins Avenue
Miami Beach, Florida 33160

Gold Coast Model & Theatrical Agency (MA)
1 Lincoln Road
Miami Beach, Florida 33139

Travis Falcon Modeling Agency (MA)
17070 Collins Avenue, Suite 233
Miami Beach, Florida 33160

North Miami

Atlantic Agency Inc. (MA)
1190 N.E. 125th Street
North Miami, Florida 33161

Beauty Talent Models (MAS)
1110 N.E. 163rd Street, Suite 211
North Miami, Florida 33162

Charm Modeling Agency (MA)
12402 B West Depre Highway
North Miami, Florida

Talent Enterprises, Inc. (MA)
1603 N.E. 123rd Street
North Miami, Florida 33161

Tampa

Barbizon of Tampa (MS)
219 Mariner Square, Suite 150
Tampa, Florida 33609

West Palm Beach

Barbizon of West Palm Beach
c/o Barbizon of Coral Gables
223 Aragon Avenue
Coral Gables, Florida

GEORGIA

Atlanta

Atlanta Models & Talent Inc. (MA)
2581 Piedmont Road, N.E.
Atlanta, Georgia 30324

Barbizon of Atlanta (MS)
100 Colony Square, Suite 300
1175 Peachtree Street, N.E.
Atlanta, Georgia 30361

Bauder Fashion College (MAS)
3355 Lenox Road, N.E.
Atlanta, Georgia 30328

Patricia Stevens Business & Fashion College (MS)
3330 Peachtree Road, N.E.
Atlanta, Georgia 30326

149

Peachtree Center Media (MA)
Atlanta Merchandise Mart, Suite 14-A-10
Atlanta, Georgia, 30303

Marietta

Chris Ann School of Charm & Modeling (MS)
808 Roswell Street, S.E.
Marietta, Georgia 30060

HAWAII

Honolulu

Barbizon of Hawaii (MS)
1600 Kapiolani Boulevard, Suite 1230
Honolulu, Hawaii 16821

ILLINOIS

Champaign

Mid-America Models (MA)
520 East Green
Champaign, Illinois 61820

Chicago

Barbizon of Chicago (MS)
John Hancock Center
875 North Michigan Avenue, Suite 1515
Chicago, Illinois 60611

Cari Scott School of Charm & Modeling (MS)
350 East 79th Street
Chicago, Illinois 60619

Chic Inc. (MA)
1207 North State Street
Chicago, Illinois 60610

Chicago School for the
  Performing Arts (MS)
7002 North Clark Street
Chicago, Illinois 60626

David Lee Models (MA)
936 North Michigan Avenue
Chicago, Illinois 60611

Eileen Slater (MA)
5445 North Sheridan Road
Chicago, Illinois 60640

The Geddes Agency (MA)
3148 Hancock Court
Chicago, Illinois 60611

Helpmate, Inc. (MA)
8 South Michigan
Chicago, Illinois 60603

Hospitality Services, Inc. (MA)
1000 North Lake Shore Drive
Chicago, Illinois 60611

John Robert Powers School (MS)
27 East Monroe
Chicago, Illinois 60603

Nover & Associates (MA)
702 North Wells
Chicago, Illinois 60610

Playboy Model Agency (MA)
919 North Michigan Avenue
Chicago, Illinois 60611

Shirley Enterprises (MA)
5244 North Magnolia
Chicago, Illinois 60640

INDIANA

Evansville

Anderson Photo Service (MA)
1008 Southern Securities Building
Evansville, Indiana 47708

Indianapolis

John Robert Powers School (MS)
7 North Meridian Street
Indianapolis, Indiana 46204

IOWA

Bettendorf

Touch of Class School of Modeling (MS)
1895 Middle Road
Bettendorf, Iowa 52722

Davenport

Ada Gaffney Shaff Modeling
  School & Agency (MAS)
310 Perry Street
Davenport, Iowa 52801

MARYLAND

Baltimore

Barbizon of Baltimore (MS)
One Investment Place
Towson, Maryland 21204

Patricia Stevens Institute of Fashion (MS)
Eastpoint Mall
Baltimore, Maryland 21228

Patricia Stevens Institute of Fashion (MS)
Westview Mall
Baltimore, Maryland 21228

Plaza Modeling & Talent Agency (MA)
205 East Joppa Road, Suite 503
Baltimore, Maryland 21204

Chevy Chase

Barbizon of Washington (MS)
5530 Wisconsin Avenue
Chevy Chase, Maryland 20015

MASSACHUSETTS

Boston

A.R.T. (MA)
69 Newbury Street
Boston, Massachusetts 02116

Academie Moderne Modeling &
Finishing School (MAS)
35 Commonwealth Avenue
Boston, Massachusetts 02116

Barbizon School of Modeling (MS)
739 Boylston Street
Boston, Massachusetts 02116

Cameo Modeling Agency (MA)
392 Boylston Street
Boston, Massachusetts 02116

Carol Nashe, Inc. (MAS)
School/Talent & Model Agency
480 Commonwealth Avenue
Boston, Massachusetts 02215

Copley 7 Models and Talent (MA)
29 Newburgh Street
Boston, Massachusetts 02116

Hart Model Agency (MA)
35 Commonwealth Avenue
Boston, Massachusetts 02116

John Robert Powers Finishing &
Modeling School (MS)
304 Boylston Street
Boston, Massachusetts 02116

Sybil, Incorporated (MA)
45 Newbury Street
Boston, Massachusetts 02117

Talent Unlimited, Ltd. (MA)
120 Boylston Street
Boston, Massachusetts 02116

The Agency for Models (MA)
31 Newbury Street
Boston, Massachusetts 02116

Dorchester

Elite Modeling Studio (MS)
663 Warren Street
Dorchester, Massachusetts 02121

South Weymouth

Carole McColes Fashion Models
School & Agency (MAS)
572 Columbian Street
South Weymouth, Massachusetts 02190

Springfield

Carol Russell Studios (MS)
20 Maple Street
Springfield, Massachusetts 01103

MICHIGAN

Dearborn

P.J. Models School & Agency (MAS)
21917 Garrison
Dearborn, Michigan 48124

Detroit

Afbony Models Agency (MAS)
2310 Cass Avenue
Detroit, Michigan 48201

Barbizon of Detroit (MS)
22255 Greenfield Road
Southfield, Michigan 48075

Gail & Rice (MA)
24455 Grand River
Detroit, Michigan 48219

Leslie Fargo Agency (MA)
811 Fisher Building
Detroit, Michigan 48202

London Studio (MA)
10095 Gratiot
Detroit, Michigan 48213

Patricia Stevens Casting Agency (MAS)
Empire Building, 107 Clifford
Detroit, Michigan 48226

Tops N Talent (MA)
307 Park Avenue Building
Detroit, Michigan 48226

Grosse Pointe

Advertisers Casting Service (MA)
15324 East Jefferson, Suite 24
Grosse Pointe, Michigan 48230

Lathrup Village

Martin-Rosenberg Talent & Model Agency (MA)
28021 Southfield Road
Lathrup Village, Michigan 48076

St. Clair Shores

Mannequin Model Agency & School (MAS)
25430 Harper Avenue
St. Clair Shores, Michigan 48081

Wyandotte

All Star Model Agency (MA)
1685 Fort Street
Wyandotte, Michigan 48192

MINNESOTA

Minneapolis

Bill Jensen Productions (MA)
3904 East 44th Street
Minneapolis, Minnesota 55406

Creative Casting Talent Agency (MA)
212 West Franklin Avenue
Minneapolis, Minnesota 55404

Eleanor Moore Model Agency, Inc. (MA)
1610-B West Lake Street
Minneapolis, Minnesota 55408

Estelle Compton Models Institute (MAS)
55 South 8th Street
Minneapolis, Minnesota 55402

Models, Photography And So Forth (MA)
1004 Marquette Avenue
Minneapolis, Minnesota 55402

Models Unlimited (MA)
309 West Lake
Minneapolis, Minnesota 55408

MISSOURI

Clayton

Barbizon School of Modeling (MAS)
7525 Forsyth Avenue
Clayton, Missouri 63105

Columbia

The Creative Eye (MA)
2207 Bear Creek Drive
Columbia, Missouri 65201

Kansas City

K.C. Metro Productions
1009 Baltimore, Suite 100
Kansas City, Missouri 64105

Raytown

Marquis Models Inc. (MA)
9804 East 87th Street
Raytown, Missouri 64138

St. Louis

Barbizon of St. Louis (MS)
Travelers Building
522 Olive Stret
St. Louis, Missouri 63101

Model Mart Agency (MAS)
9500 Page Boulevard
St. Louis, Missouri 63132

John Robert Powers School (MS)
111 South Meramec
St. Louis, Missouri 63105

NEBRASKA

Omaha

Bell School of Modeling (MAS)
4441 North 63rd Street
Omaha, Nebraska 68104

Dory Passolt Models (MAS)
1330 North 95th Street
Omaha, Nebraska 68114

Nancy Bounds Model–Charm School
   & Agency (MAS)
4803 Davenport
Omaha, Nebraska 68132

Patricia Stevens Fashion & Secretarial
   College (MS)
117 North 32nd Avenue
Omaha, Nebraska 68131

NEW JERSEY

Atlantic City

Atlantic City School of Modeling (MAS)
Convention Hall, 2337 Pacifica
Atlantic City, New Jersey 08401

Haddonfield

The Richmond Models
223 Kings Highway East
Haddonfield, New Jersey 08033

Highland Park

Barbizon of Highland Park (MS)
Park Professional Building
300 Raritan Avenue
Highland Park, New Jersey 08904

Montclair

Barbizon of Montclair (MS)
70 Park Street
Montclair, New Jersey 07042

Paramus

Barbizon of Bergen (MS)
S-10 Route 17 at Route 4
Paramus, New Jersey 07652

Red Bank

Barbizon of Red Bank (MS)
188 East Bergen Place
Red Bank, New Jersey 07701

Trenton

Barbizon of Trenton (MS)
1911 Princeton Avenue
Trenton, New Jersey 08033

Union

Barbizon of Union (MS)
2816 Morris Avenue
Union, New Jersey 07083

Wyckoff

Patricia Rainey Agency, Inc. (MA)
175 Fox Hollow Road
Wyckoff, New Jersey 07481

NEW YORK

Babylon

Barbizon of Babylon (MS)
8 Little East Neck Road
Babylon, L.I., New York 11702

Bellmore

Studio One Enterprises (MAS)
P.O. Box 34
Bellmore, New York 11710

Buffalo

Barbizon of Buffalo (MS)
Statler Hilton Hotel
Niagara Square
Buffalo, New York 14202

John Robert Powers School (MS)
300 Delaware Avenue
Buffalo, New York 14202

New York City

Barbizon School of Modeling (MAS)
689 Fifth Avenue
New York, New York 10022

Black Beauty Inc. (MA)
(Black and Hispanic only)
145 East 52nd Street
New York, New York 10017

Filor Talent Agency (MA)
110 East 55th Street
New York, New York 10022

Ford Models (MA)
344 East 59th Street
New York, New York 10022

Foster-Fell Agency, Inc. (MA)
515 Madison Avenue
New York, New York 10022

Ellen Harth, Inc. (MA)
515 Madison Avenue
New York, New York 10022

Perkins Agency—TV (MA)
139 East 52nd Street
New York, New York 10022

Stewart Models (MA)
405 Park Avenue
New York, New York 10022

Stone Models (MA)
527 Madison Avenue
New York, New York 10022

Wilhelmina Models (MA)
9 East 37th Street
New York, New York 10016

William Schuller Agency (MA)
667 Madison Avenue
New York, New York 10021

Zoli (MA)
121 East 62nd Street
New York, New York 10021

Rego Park, Queens

Barbizon of Queens (MS)
95-20 63rd Road
Rego Park, Queens, New York 11374

Rochester

Barbizon of Rochester (MS)
850 Powers Building
Rochester, New York 14614

John Robert Powers School (MS)
133 East Avenue
Rochester, New York 14618

Syracuse

Barbizon of Syracuse (MS)
351 South Warren Street
Syracuse, New York 13202

White Plains

Barbizon of Westchester (MS)
White Plains Hotel
South Broadway & Lyon Place
White Plains, New York 10601

NEVADA

Las Vegas

Fashion Merchandising Institute of Nevada (MS)
1456 East Charleston Boulevard
Las Vegas, Nevada 89104

Georgie Girl Industries, Inc. (MA)
Circus Drive at Box 14012
Las Vegas, Nevada 89114

Universal Models (MA)
953 East Sahara #27B
Las Vegas, Nevada 89109

NEW HAMPSHIRE

Manchester

Cinderella Modeling Studios (MA)
9 Brook Street
Manchester, New Hampshire 03104

NORTH CAROLINA

Charlotte

Libby Stone Finishing & Modeling School (MAS)
2425 Chesterfield Avenue
Charlotte, North Carolina 28205

TRIM, Troyance Ross Institution
   of Modeling (MAS)
600 Queens Road
Charlotte, North Carolina 28207

Greensboro

The Beauty Spot (MAS)
P.O. Box 9502
Greensboro, North Carolina 27408

Raleigh

John Robert Powers (MS)
3522 Haworth Drive, Suite 101
Raleigh, North Carolina 27609

OHIO

Cincinnati

Kathleen Wellman School of
  Fashion and Modeling (MAS)
One One East Fourth Building
Cincinnati, Ohio 45202

Lillian Galloway School of
  Modeling, Inc. (MAS)
Cincinnati Model Agency
7784 Montgomery Road
Cincinnati, Ohio 45236

Limelight Associates (MA)
Professional Model Agency
3560 Bayard Drive
Cincinnati, Ohio 45208

Urbane Academy (MS)
22 West 7th Street
Cincinnati, Ohio 45202

VIVA Agency (MA)
Models – Talent
22 West 7th Street
Cincinnati, Ohio 45202

Cleveland

Barbizon School of Cleveland (MAS)
110 Terminal Tower
Cleveland, Ohio 44113

David Lee Models (MA)
325 Cleveland Plaza
Cleveland, Ohio 44115

Powers Models (MS)
1258 Euclid Avenue
Cleveland, Ohio 44115

Columbus

Wright Models (MA)
4100 North High Street
Columbus, Ohio 43214

Lancaster

Abbott Charm School & Model Agency (MAS)
Equitable Building, Suite 308
Lancaster, Ohio 43130

Youngstown

Barbizon of Youngstown (MS)
The Legal Arts Building, Suite 505
101 Market Street
Youngstown, Ohio 44503

OKLAHOMA

Oklahoma City

Park Avenue Modeling School (MAS)
3919 North Pennsylvania, Suite 100
Oklahoma City, Oklahoma 73112

Tulsa

Sherack Studio Model Agency & School
  of Photography (MAS)
1727 South Cheyenne
Tulsa, Oklahoma 74119

OREGON

Eastside

Golden Girl School of Self Improvement
  & Modeling (MS)
23 Cypress Point
Eastside, Oregon 97420

Portland

Caryl Edeline School of Acting &
  Modeling (MS)
1969 N.E. 42nd Street
Portland, Oregon 97213

John Robert Powers School (MS)
203 S.W. 9th Avenue
Portland, Oregon 97205

PENNSYLVANIA

Emmaus

Jan Nogy School (MS)
1011 Pennsylvania Avenue
Emmaus, Pennsylvania 18049

Jenkintown

Eastern Models Association (MA)
417 Old York Road
Jenkintown, Pennsylvania 19046

Philadelphia

Barbizon School of Modeling (MAS)
1520 Walnut Street
Philadelphia, Pennsylvania 19102

International Modeling Guild, Inc. (MAS)
1730 Chestnut Street
Philadelphia, Pennsylvania 19103

John Robert Powers (MS)
1425 Chestnut Street
Philadelphia, Pennsylvania 19103

Ruth Harper's Modeling and Charm School (MAS)
1427 West Erie Avenue
Philadelphia, Pennsylvania 19140

Studio Guild of Professional Models (MA)
1126 Walnut Street
Philadelphia, Pennsylvania 19107

Pittsburgh

Barbizon School of Modeling (MS)
Gateway Towers
Pittsburgh, Pennsylvania 15222

Kip Models Agency (MAS)
Cathredral Mansions
4716 Ellsworth Avenue
Pittsburgh, Pennsylvania 15213

Models Unlimited (MA)
290 Gateway Towers
Pittsburgh, Pennsylvania 15222

Powers Career School (MAS)
100 Fifth Avenue
Pittsburgh, Pennsylvania 15222

Pat Lyon
Wheeler Agency (MAS)
William Penn Hotel
Pittsburgh, Pennsylvania 15219

RHODE ISLAND

Providence

Barbara Model Agency (MA)
279 Benefit Street
Providence, Rhode Island 02903

Barbizon of Providence (MS)
302 Union Trust Building
170 Westminister Street
Providence, Rhode Island 02903

North Providence

Barbara Model Agency
Barbara School of Charm & Modeling (MAS)
1115 Mineral Spring Avenue
North Providence, Rhode Island 02904

SOUTH CAROLINA

Columbia

Fashion Merchandising School of
  Columbia Commercial College (MS)
Suite 209 Dutch Plaza
800 Dutch Square Boulevard
Columbia, South Carolina 29210

Millie Lewis Modeling School &
  Agency (MAS)
3022 Milwood Avenue
Columbia, South Carolina 29205

Greenville

Millie Lewis Modeling Agency
Diran Executive Plaza
850 South Pleasantburg Drive
Greenville, South Carolina 29607

TEXAS

Corpus Christi

Modeling & Finishing School of
  Corpus Christi (MS)
5333 Everhart, Suite 165
Corpus Christi, Texas 78411

Dallas

Barbizon School of Modeling of Dallas (MAS)
1200 Main Street, Suite 1200
Dallas, Texas 75202

Joan Frank Models (MA)
Suite 228
Two Turtle Creek Village
Dallas, Texas 75219

Kim Dawson Agency (MA)
1143 Apparel Mart
Dallas, Texas 75207

Miss Wade's Fashion Merchandise College (MAS)
59500 Apparel Mart
Dallas, Texas 75207

Peggy Taylor Talent, Inc. (MA)
4228 North Central Expressway
Dallas, Texas 75206

Story Book Playhouse (MA)
505 Golden Triangle
Dallas, Texas 75224

Tanya Blair Agency (MA)
2320 North Griffin
Dallas, Texas 75202

Deer Park

Ga'Sondra's School of Modeling (MS)
1202 Velma
Deer Park, Texas 77536

El Paso

Barbizon School of Modeling & Fashion (MS)
801 North Stanton Street
El Paso, Texas 79901

Houston

CC & Company (MA)
P.O. #35755
Houston, Texas 77072

Fashion IV (MS)
3935 Westheimer
Houston, Texas 77027

K. Winters Agency & School of
  Modeling
314 Camino South Shopping Center
Houston, Texas 77062

"Mad Hatter" (MA)
10264 Hammerly
Houston, Texas 77043

Studio Venus (MA)
505 Sul Ross
Houston, Texas 77006

WASHINGTON

Seattle

The Carolyn Hasen Agency (MAS)
1516 Sixth Avenue
Seattle, Washington 98101

Elizabeth Leonard School of Charm
  & Modeling (MAS)
4th & Pike
Seattle, Washington 98101

John Robert Powers (MAS)
1610 Sixth Avenue
Seattle, Washington 98101

Kathleen Peck Finishing School/
  Model Agency (MAS)
716 White-Henry-Stuart Building
Seattle, Washington 98101

Standard Artist Management (MA)
18601 Pacific Highway South
Suite 205
Seattle, Washington 98188

Thompson Teen & Top Models (MAS)
11522 24th Street, N.E.
Seattle, Washington 98125
(Three other schools in surburban
Seattle, N.,S.,E.)

WASHINGTON, D.C.

Barre Finishing & Modeling School (MAS)
National Press Building
529 14th Street, N.W.
Washington, D.C. 20004

Cappa Chell School & Model Agency (MAS)
1739 Connecticut Avenue, N.W.
Washington, D.C. 20009

PUERTO RICO

San Juan

Barbizon of San Juan (MS)
El Caribe Building
Fifth Avenue
San Juan, Puerto Rico 00901
809-724-1112

CANADA

BRITISH COLUMBIA

Vancouver

Elizabeth Leslie, Ltd. (MAS)
1102 Hornby Street
Vancouver, B.C., CANADA
604-681-7245

Pacific Show Productions, Ltd. (MA)
1122 925 W. Georgia Street
Vancouver, B.C., V6C 1R5, CANADA
604-681-0021

Ramona Beauchamp Model Agency (MAS)
2033 W. 42nd Avenue
Vancouver, B.C., CANADA
604-266-5555

ONTARIO

Brampton

Jennifer Walmsley Modeling
   School (MAS)
338 Queen Street East, Suite 204
Brampton, Ontario, CANADA
416-457-8373

Toronto

Barbizon of Toronto (MS)
360 Bay Street
Toronto 105, Ontario, CANADA
416-367-1386

Joy Davies (MAS)
P.O. Box 699 – Station "F"
Toronto, Ontario M4Y 2N6, CANADA
416-368-1191

Nicholas Harvey Modeling Agency (MAS)
20 Prince Arthur Avenue
Toronto, Ontario
416-962-7297

Elaine Phillips Productions (MAS)
44 Jackes Aufrathe
Apartment 1809
Toronto, Ontario, M4T 1E5, CANADA
416-964-1490

Eleanor Fulcher, Ltd. (MAS)
667 Yonge Street
Toronto, Ontario, CANADA
416-924-9633

Jerry Lodge Talent Agency
   (& Model Division)
Bette Milne Model Agency (MAS)
64 Merton Street
Toronto, Ontario, M4S 1A1
Lodge: 416-486-4500
Milne: 416-486-4610

London of England Academy (MAS)
17 Prince Arthur Avenue
Toronto, Ontario
416-923-8956

Judy Welch (MAS)
224 Bloor Street West
Toronto, Ontario
416-924-7474

Walter Thornton Model Agency
   & School (MAS)
60 Avenue Road
Toronto, Ontario M5R 2H1
416-923-0961
416-923-4629

Williams Model Service (MA)
574 Yonge Street
Suite 6
Toronto, Ontario M54Y 1Y1
416-961-1448

QUEBEC

Montreal

Audrey Morris, Ltd. (MA)
Place Benaventure
Montreal, Quebec
514-866-1167

Barton-Taylor (MAS)
1470 Peel Street
Suite 903
Montreal, Quebec H3A 1T1
514-284-3666

Constance Brown, Ltd. (MA)
3465 Cote des Neiges
Montreal, Quebec
514-934-0393

EUROPEAN MODEL AGENCIES

ENGLAND

London

Peter Benison
91 Shaftesbury Avenue
London, W.1., England

Lucie Clayton
66 New Bond Street
London, W1Y OAT, England

International Model Agency
7 Duke Street
London, W.1., England

London Model Agency
43 Charlotte Street
London, W.1., England

Models One
200 Fulham Road
London, S.W. 10, England

Nev's Agency
18 Coulson Street
London, S.W.3, England

Top Models Ltd.
37 Percy Street
London, W.1., England

Whittaker Enterprises Ltd.
33 Brook Street
London, W.1., England

FRANCE

Paris

Agence Stephanie D'Avray
76 Champs Elysees
Paris, France

Christa Modeling
9 Rue Keppler
Paris, France

Euro Planning
3 Rue de Courcelles
Paris, France

International Model
21 Rue du Cirque
Paris, France

Models International
3 Avenue Victor Hugo
Paris, France

Modeling International
6 Avenue de Breteuil
Paris, France

Pauline's Model Agency
47 Rue de l'Arbe
Paris, France

Top Models
3 Rue de L'Arrivee
Paris, France

ITALY

Rome

Donatella Mauro
Via Citta di Castello, 35
Rome, Itlay 00191

Top Floor Agency
Via Angelo Brunetti, 47
Rome, Italy 00186

Milan

Donatella Mauro
Via Alberto da Giussano, 1a
Milan, Italy 20154

Fashion Models
Via Seprio, 2
Milan, Italy 20149

Jet Models
Via Zuratti, 54
Milan, Italy 20125

Studio 70
Via Mellerio, 3
Milan, Italy 20123